Praise for *Singing to A Bulldog*

"Anson has a genius for telling stories. *Singing to A Bulldog* is a heartwarming autobiography based on the inspirational life lessons Anson learned in the course of his unlikely friendship with Willie [Turner]. Throughout Anson's spectacular career as an actor, director, musician, and entrepreneur, Willie's wisdom has served him well, giving him the confidence to move forward and take on new challenges.

—**Sheila Weidenfeld, former press secretary to
Betty Ford and Special Assistant to President Gerald Ford**

"I just read this delightful debut book and thoroughly enjoyed every page. *Singing To A Bulldog* is an inspiring, heartwarming look into Anson Williams's career as he candidly reveals the youthful challenges and insecurities that might have kept him from an impressive future were it not for Willie Turner, the man who would dispel those doubts and teach him to 'stop looking at the mountain, and go climb it!' The genuine appreciation for the mentor who motivated Anson to embrace his future is refreshing, and that gratitude is the connecting thread that weaves through Anson's story."

—**Ann Jillian**

"I loved the book. . . . [E]xtraordinary: It is not only a 'how to succeed' look at accomplishing professional goals but also a philosophical teaching of how to achieve a successful and contributory life."

—**Barbara Boyle, Associate Dean,
Entrepreneurship and Special Initiatives, UCLA**

SINGING TO A BULLDOG

*From "Happy Days" to Hollywood
Director, and the Unlikely Mentor
Who Got Me There*

ANSON WILLIAMS

The Reader's Digest Association, Inc.
New Yok, NY • Montreal

A READER'S DIGEST BOOK

Copyright © 2014 Anson Williams

Cover photo: © ABC Photo Archives

ISBN 978-1-62145-225-6

Library of Congress Cataloging-in-Publication Data
Williams, Anson.
  Singing to a bulldog : from "Happy days" to Hollywood director, and the unlikely mentor who got me there / by Anson Williams.
    pages cm
  ISBN 978-1-62145-225-6 (alk. paper) -- ISBN 978-1-62145-226-3 (epub) 1. Williams, Anson. 2. Actors--United States--Biography. 3. Television producers and directors--United States--Biography. I. Title.
  PN2287.W4597A3 2015
  791.4502'8092--dc23
  [B]
                          2014033450

We are committed to both the quality of our products and the service we provide to our customers. We value your comments, so please feel free to contact us.

          The Reader's Digest Association, Inc.
          Adult Trade Publishing
          44 South Broadway
          White Plains, NY 10601

For more Reader's Digest products and information, visit our website:

          www.rd.com (in the United States)
          www.readersdigest.ca (in Canada)

Printed in the United States of America

1 3 5 7 9 10 8 6 4 2

*This book is dedicated to everyone who needs
Willie Turner's life lessons to stop looking at their
mountain and to start climbing it.*

Contents

INTRODUCTION

"You gonna do somethin' great in life. Just a feelin' I got."

These are the words that changed my life. They came from my boss, Willie Turner, head janitor for Leonard's Department Store, located in Burbank, California. It was the end of my first day of work as his assistant janitor. I'd just finished cleaning up the women's restroom, and was putting the supplies away in what Willie called, "Dey Talk Room," a small janitorial space with a couple of rusted–out oil drum cans to sit on. Willie pulled out his flask of Jack Daniel's and took a few swallows. "Sit down, boy," he said.

Nervously I sat on a drum, the smell of whiskey filling the closet-sized room, and waited for the words "You fired, boy." I was used to failing. My dad made sure of it. Every day of my fifteen years on this planet I was told, "If it wasn't for you, I'd have my own art gallery, wouldn't have to feed your stupid face." Dad made damn sure that his failure was my failure, and I made damn sure that he wasn't let down: I was irresponsible, insecure, klutzy—a real poster boy for disappointment. Willie took one last hit of whiskey before sitting down next to me on the other drum. We both just sat there for a moment.

"Damn good job. Like you, boy."

Confused, I turned to him. "Huh?"

Willie burst out laughing at my insightful response, his smile brightening up the room. Finally, I just had to join in, laughing more with him in a minute than in my entire fifteen years. Willie had a way of making me feel good.

"You funny!" he shouted out through his hilarity.

Catching my breath, I asked, "Why?"

Settling down, Willie enjoyed another good swig. "You just funny, boy."

"Didn't mean to be," I replied.

Putting away his flask, Willie got up and grabbed a pack of cigarettes from a grease-stained jacket. "Dat's why you funny." Lighting up, he sat back down. "You did good today, gonna work out fine."

I couldn't help smiling. "Thanks."

Willie kept looking at me, as if he really knew me, my future, everything. Never taking his kind eyes off me, he leaned over and put his worn hand on my shoulder.

"You special, boy. You gonna do somethin' great in life. Got a feelin'."

And that was the beginning. I was a wreck of a kid sitting on an old rusty oil drum; yet I became an international television star, dated the daughter of the President of the United States, spent a day with John Lennon, sang for Elvis, wrote, directed, and produced for television, and launched a successful product company. All because an aging African American janitor saw some magic in me, and took the time to share his wisdom. I listened, and it was the best thing I ever did, because Willie's advice cut through all the noise in my life and gave me the confidence to move forward, and helped me find . . . me. My name is on this book yet I promise you, without Willie I'd have no stories to tell. Willie was uneducated, in his fifties, and had a serious drinking problem—but if I had judged him because of his unglamorous job or his failings, I would have missed getting advice from the one person most able to help me turn my life around. Of all the things Willie Turner taught me, not judging was the most important. In my experience, our real heroes are not making billions of dollars, trending on the Internet, or posing on magazine covers. They're "ordinary" people, sent here as extraordinary messengers to help us find the answers we are seeking and the path to our truest selves—if we don't judge by appearances, and instead listen to their words of enlightenment.

You Sing Okay, Can't Dance for Sh*t

" All good, boy. Don't gets in dey way of yerself.
Go wit yer feelins."

Both of my parents grew up during the Depression and felt the pangs of not having food on the table. Security meant the world to them, which meant that I was going to be a teacher, engineer, civil service worker—anything that offered abundant job opportunities. In our house, the word "entertainer" was a surefire, E-ticket ride out the door. When I told them I wanted to be a performer, they opened the front door of our home wide. "Come back when you get some sense," were their last spoken words as my butt hit the street.

★ ★ ★

I was twenty years old, a part-time student, a full-time shoe salesman, and a crooner of songs at four talent nights a week in Los Angeles. My showbiz career had earned me minus $200 (it took gas to get to the unpaid gigs).

One night at Jack Calley's, a restaurant and bar that had a Tuesday talent night, a waiter and aspiring actor, Jimmy Donald, told me about an open call. It was a summer stock audition that was going to be held at the Masonic Temple in Hollywood. He said it started at 10 a.m., but that I should get there early to secure a good place in line. If you haven't heard of it, "summer stock" is a term used for a season of stage musicals; typically, they feature a different star in each show and use a stock company of performers who can perform in them all. My total "professional" show biz experience up to that moment was singing songs to a crowd of white-collar alcoholics and aged hookers looking for business. I had never done a theater audition, but Jimmy assured me that it was nothing, saying to "just bring some sheet music."

The next morning, I searched the one-bedroom flop house I lived in with three other smelly, loser friends—I was hunting for sticky, loose change that I desperately needed for gas. I got down to the Masonic Temple by 8 a.m. It looked like a Pharaoh's palace, and there were already hundreds of assorted Hollyweird humans standing in two separate lines around the building. Why are there two lines? I wondered.

It turned out that one line was for Equity members and the other for non-Equity. Actor's Equity Association (AEA or often simply Equity) is a union for live theater. This particular audition was open to both union and nonunion actors.

The Equity line went first. My line stood in the sun and sweated profusely. We didn't move for hours. Finally, after I had sweat staining every inch of my clothing, the non–Equity line started moving. Our line went much faster—from where I was standing, it seemed that no sooner had a person entered the building than they were walking right out. As I got closer to the entrance, I could hear voices belting out show tunes. I'd hear around eight bars and then the voice would suddenly stop. A moment later, another voice, and then another, and so on, as a steady stream of rejected faces slouched out the door and back into their regular lives.

At last, it was my turn to enter the massive lobby. The building was beyond intimidating, as if its purpose was to make all who entered feel small and insignificant. The voices belting songs were louder now, though each was quickly silenced. As I got closer to the audition room and saw the rejected, dejected hopefuls walking in the opposite direction, I desperately wanted to bolt back into my parents' arms. I would promise to become anything that they wanted me to be. What stopped me from doing this was Willie. I felt his calming hand on my shoulder and heard his words, "All good boy. Don't gets in dey way of yerself. Go wit yer feelins."

Willie had died from alcoholism a year earlier, but he'd never really left me.

One more dispirited body rushed out the door and then it was my turn to enter the audition room. The door opened and I willed myself forward. I found myself standing in another massive room where I saw a long, beat-up table and three sour faces. In the corner was a crappy piano, and on the bench was a craggy-looking player with a lit Marlboro cigarette hanging from his lips. He said, "Give me your music."

Nerve-wracked, I handed him the sheet music to the song, "Mame."

I looked over at the lifeless threesome as the opening bars of "Mame" started filling the room, echoing off the walls. I

start to sing—*You coax the blues right out of the horn, Mame*—
and immediately forgot the words. Without missing a beat, I
instinctively began making up my own: *You charm my tux right
off in the morn', Mame.* The three zombie faces grinned. I kept
on singing whatever sprang to mind and fit the beat, and their
chuckles turned into unadulterated guffaws. I didn't think it
was a good sign, but my memory wasn't catching up to the
tune, and I didn't want to stop. I carried on as the laughter
grew, until even the prune-faced piano man was howling.

I sang the whole song to the end. The group behind the
long table settled down, wiped tears from their eyes, and the
man in the middle chair asked my name.

"Anson Williams," I answered.

"Do you dance, Anson?"

I started to say, "No," but stopped myself. I remembered
Willie saying, "You different, boy. Gotta show dat."

"Sure," I said.

"Okay, once we finish up the singing auditions, we'll
bring you back in with rest of the callbacks for the dance
part."

"Callbacks?" I questioned.

Laughing, he said, "Performers that we want to see again."

Stunned, I stammered, "You want to see me?"

"Wait outside," he said, and motioned for the next victim
to walk in.

I think I waited for a full hour before the singing auditions finally finished. Out of all of the hopefuls waiting
in both lines early that morning, the group in the Pharaoh's
throne room was whittled down to thirty callbacks. It turned
out that auditions were being done in New York, Chicago,

and Los Angeles to cast a resident company in Wichita, Kansas. Cast members would be chosen (and contracts signed) right on the spot.

The door of the audition room opened and the youngest looking member of the audition panel walked out. "Everybody listen up. My name is Fredrick, and I'll be teaching you the routine. Please follow me."

We all followed him into another large room. This one sported mirrors across the entire front wall. I had a hard enough time just walking and talking, so I purposely found a spot in back that was hidden from the mirrored surveillance. It didn't take long before I had that "bolt-to-mommy" feeling again. It was horrifyingly clear to me that everyone in that room was a trained dancer: They were jumping, leaping, twisting, and twirling, all in perfect unison. I was not. No one ever accused me of being a good dancer; and learning a Bob Fosse *Sweet Charity* routine in less than 15 minutes? What were the odds? "Gotta' show you different" rang through my head. "I'll do that, Willie," I whispered to myself.

The session soon ended; we were split into two groups, and Fredrick took my group back into the audition room. My instincts took over and this time I made damn sure that I was in the front row as the *Sweet Charity* music started to swell. The dancers in the room moved in perfect synchronization. But not me: When they were all jumping, I made sure I was turning. When they were twirling, I was jumping. If they were moving, I was standing still, listening to the guffaws from the table. The music ended with an almost-perfect group "ta dah!" and me sliding into home. There were gut laughs from the auditors.

Finally, the man in the middle spoke up again. He asked three people to wait outside. "The rest of you are dismissed."

Dejected, I walked toward the door as he went to huddle with the others at the table.

"Anson!" he shouted after me. "Wait outside too."

I get to wait! The phoenix had risen!

Then the second group went in and two more people were asked to stay. They had their five people. Why was I still waiting? Then I knew: Uh oh! I bet that they want to tell me not to think about auditioning ever again. For anything. Yeah, that's it. I wasn't serious enough. I'm through.

I waited nervously as the five lucky ones finalized their summer employment. Ecstatic, they ran out of the building, leaving me alone, a shoe salesman in a Pharaoh's domain. The door abruptly opened and the piano player, cigarette still smoking between his nicotine-stained lips, walked out. I could swear he gave me a wink as he passed by. Then I heard, "Anson?"

I turned and there was Fredrick. "Come on in."

I walked back into the room. The middle man pointed to an empty seat. "Sit down."

I did as I was told.

"My name's Frank Kenley. I'm the show producer."

I sat in silence, waiting for certain rejection.

"You sing okay; you can't dance for shit," Frank continued. "But you've got something. You're different."

My skin literally tingled, and I could feel Willie's smile lighting up the room.

"We have an apprentice program. You would be in every show, help build the sets, basically work your ass off fifteen hours a day, seven days a week. For that we'll pay you fifty dollars a week plus your room and board. If you do a great job, we'll sign you to an Equity contract your last show, and you'll be able to join the union as a professional."

I was stunned. "You're going to pay me?" That's the only thing I could think to say.

As I left that day, I felt large in the Pharaoh's tiny palace. I had my first paying gig. Why? Because I didn't get in the way of myself.

Bingo Clubs and Retirement Home Escapees

*"You don't looks at a mountain, you climbs.
Dat's who wins, boy."*

My summer stock experience was akin to unsanctioned torture: up at 5 a.m., build sets, paint flats, build sets, rehearse,
paint flats, perform, build sets, paint flats, and get to bed by
1 a.m. However, it did gift me with an Equity card, which
is the Holy Grail. I was now a professional, and that meant I
was privileged to stand on the "Equity side" of audition lines.
The lines were still never-ending, but one of them landed me
a replacement job in an original musical comedy titled *Victory
Canteen*. Milt Larsen and Bobby Lauher wrote the script and
the score was by the Sherman Brothers, famous for the music
in the film version of *Mary Poppins*. Wow! I thought. I am
now one of the stars of a major musical right here in the heart
of Hollywood! Every major player in the world of entertain-

ment will see me and offer me representation. I will be signed by a powerful agent and get fantastic jobs. I have made it!

There was only one problem: No players came. We played to packed houses consisting of bingo clubs and retirement home escapees. After several weeks of this, I was more than disappointed. The cast had warned me, but I didn't believe them. Looking out at our audiences *I* was ready to retire; no one in those seats was going to come backstage after the show and hand me a golden key to Hollywood success. Then one morning a long-lost Willie moment found its way into my brain. "You don't looks at a mountain, you climbs. Dat's who wins, boy."

So instead of quitting, I decided to climb. Grabbing the phone book, I looked up the addresses of the three largest and most powerful talent agencies I knew of: William Morris Agency (WMA), Creative Management Agency (CMA), and IFA Talent. The closest to my apartment was IFA, so I (metaphorically) tied up my hiking boots, jumped into my beat up old Corvair (they don't exist anymore), and headed for the mountain—which in this case was in Beverly Hills, California.

The agency represented major stars of the era: Jane Fonda, Charlton Heston, and Marlon Brando were a few of the bold letter names. Not wanting to spend a rent payment on parking, I found a spot at least a half a mile from the building and then hoofed it to Mount IFA. The building itself was imposing: a grand monument to the already successful. I took the elevator to the fifth floor. When the elevator doors opened, I found myself in a large, impeccably decorated lobby. At the far end, beckoning me, were large, gold letters: I F A. They gleamed on the wall behind the glamorous-looking young receptionist. I felt like I was approaching The Great Oz as I walked toward this starlet-to-be.

"I'd like to see an agent," I said.

"Do you have a name?" she responded.

"Anyone's fine," I answered.

"You need a name," she said with attitude, "and an appointment." She then turned away rudely and took a call. I just stood there, not sure what the hell to do.

"You climbs. Dat's who wins, boy."

I decided to sit my ass down on a couch and wait. The receptionist finished her call and turned, locking devil eyes on me. "You have to leave, sir."

This time, I turned away from her.

"Did you hear me? I said that you have to leave."

"That's okay," I said, looking back at her. "I'll just sit here until an agent's free."

Evil Starlet threatened to call security, then the police, but I didn't budge.

I sat there for hours. Periodically she would dial and whisper into her phone. I wondered if she was organizing a firing squad. Then I heard, "You! Hey you!"

I glanced toward the voice. A young guy in a suit was holding open a door that led out of the waiting room. He was looking in my direction. "Me?" I said.

"Yeah, you. Get over here."

I jumped up and pretty much leaped across the room. "Are you an agent?"

"Yes."

That was all I needed to hear. He held the key to my future, my mountain's plateau! An agent! I started telling him about me, the show—

"I got it," he interrupted, "Follow me."

I made sure to give a princess wave to the "witch" before entering the Emerald City. I followed my future agent into his small office; at that moment it seemed as big as the Taj Mahal. I continued to excitedly sell my wares.

"Alright!" he interrupted again. "Can I say something?"

Startled, I shut up.

He told me that he had just received a casting breakdown for a segment of a Universal show called *Owen Marshall, Counselor at Law*. They needed actors that were over eighteen years old who could portray high school football players. IFA didn't have any clients that fit the bill. He heard about a pain-in-the-ass kid who was doing a sit-down strike in the lobby, so he decided to take a look. Cutting to the chase, he said he would take a shot, and book me for an audition the next morning. If I got the job, he would sign me to the agency.

I floated back to my car. "I got a 10 a.m. meeting with Jon Epstein! I got a 10 a.m. meeting with Jon Epstein!" were the words dancing through my head. He was a television producer! He was the man who would change my life!

I made sure to arrive at Jon Epstein's office an hour early the next morning. It was a good thing I did, because his secretary handed me a scene in which a football player dies from a drug overdose. I read this scene with mounting panic: I was auditioning for this particular football player and, yes, it was his death scene. All of my show biz experience leading to this moment was earned in light-hearted musicals; I'd never even had an acting lesson. The closest that I'd ever come to a death scene was watching Olivia Hussey in *Romeo and Juliet*. I was finished before I started.

"Don't gets in dey way of yerself." I heard Willie's comforting voice, and it calmed me down. "Feelins is truth." His words changed me—I walked over to a chair, sat down, and started studying the scene in earnest. Feelings are truth. I started thinking about my childhood dog, Shatzie, who died in my arms, and those painful feelings came roaring back. Willie had given me the most important tool for acting: connection.

At exactly 10 a.m. I was ushered into a large, comfy office with deep shag carpeting. Three people were in the room— Jon Epstein, the man that I thought could change my life, a casting director who would read the scene with me, and a skinny, young guy with glasses standing in the corner. I had no idea what his purpose was; only the other two introduced themselves.

The audition started and I did the scene as realistically as I could; I damn well died on Jon Epstein's plush carpeting. When I got back on my feet, I found out he had nothing to do with the show's casting. That was up to the young man with glasses. His name was Steven Spielberg. He was already on the road to greatness, and had stopped directing television at this stage of his career. But Jon Epstein was his friend, and when a director suddenly dropped out of the episode, Spielberg graciously agreed to help him out.

The shoot itself went as well as the audition. To date it is the only death scene I've played in my career. And the best part? The next Saturday night, my new agent from one of the world's largest talent agencies came to see me—and the entire cast—in *Victory Canteen*. It wasn't a television producer who changed my life, or even Steven Spielberg. It was a wise janitor who gave me the push I needed to climb my mountain.

LESSON 3

What's a Potsie?

"Some things supposed to be. Make you go different ways; better ways to get dere."

After being signed by IFA and "dying" on camera with Steven Spielberg, master of film, behind the lens, landing a regular paycheck in show biz appeared feasible. My agent started booking me in parts that I began to think of collectively as "Concerned Boyfriend" roles. On each job, every other actor in my scenes would converse, and then I would react appropriately until I said my line, "I understand." A scene could be five pages long and all I'd be responsible for was those two words, plus expert head turning and nodding. Still, it was a living, and soon I could actually afford a place on my own.

After two years of playing the Concerned Boyfriend in different venues, and perfecting head nods of understanding, I received a call from my agent.

"Hey Anson, you've got an audition today," he said. "It's

SINGING TO A BULLDOG

a pilot about the fifties, called *Happy Days*, and they can't find a guy for one of the leads. It films in two days."

I took down the info and got ready as quickly as I could; I had to be at Paramount Studios in less than two hours. I jumped into my aged Corvair and felt revved up. I had never auditioned for a series pilot before! I hit the gas and was on my way. Then many miles away from the audition a bogey-man chose its moment to sneak into my engine: My car lost power, forcing me to the side of the road. I could not believe my luck. I didn't know anything about car engines. To make things worse, the heavens opened in sunny California, and it started to pour down rain.

At the time, cell phones only existed if you were on *Star Trek*. I wasn't, so my only option was to get out of the traitorous Corvair, sluice my way through the gale, and find a phone. Which is what I did. I ran through the rain to a payphone and called AAA. They informed me that there were a lot of road problems at the moment, and that they would get to me as soon as they could. Then they hung up. I listened to the dial tone and watched as it began raining even harder. I practically swam back to my vehicle. Only once I was back inside it did the thought occur to me: I should have called my agent! I should have, but there was no way I was leaving the womb of my car again. I was sure my chance at the pilot was gone.

It took almost two hours for AAA to arrive. The fix was a simple one: A cable had detached from my battery. Ready to turn around for home, I thought of what Willie told me once when I felt that I had unfairly lost a position on my high school football team. "Some things supposed to be. Make you go different ways; better ways to get dere, boy." I decided to keep heading for Paramount Studios.

When I arrived, I was both relieved and surprised to learn that my name was still at the gate. As pitiful as I must have looked, they let me through. It was still pissing rain when I finally found the office of Millie Gussie, the head of casting. Soaking wet and dripping on the reception area carpet, I announced my name to her secretary, who looked me up and down without saying a word and then buzzed Millie.

"It sure as hell is about time he got here!" I heard from somewhere beyond the waiting area. Then out walked a short, no-nonsense lady, cigarette in hand. She stopped short. "What the hell happened to you?"

I quickly explained as she virtually kicked my ass into her office. "You're damn lucky," Millie said, "that we still haven't found the actor for Potsie."

"What's a Potsie?" I asked.

"Look this over quickly," she answered, handing me a script. "And then read where it's marked."

I started reading and immediately thought of Howie Shertzman, one of my best friends growing up. A little gullible and awkward socially, he was Potsie. I read with Millie, doing my best Howie impersonation.

Without any expression, she said, "Wait here."

She walked into another office, but didn't close the door all the way. "I don't care if you're looking at wardrobe," I could hear her phone conversation. "He's perfect. Get the hell down here now." Walking back in, she said, "Wait outside. Garry Marshall, the executive producer, is coming down to see you."

I did as I was told. I reread the script and studied it for about ten minutes before a haggard-looking man walked straight past me into Millie's office. She closed the door and then opened it a few minutes later. "Come on," she said, waving me over.

I walked in, and the man who would change my life forever said, "I'm Garry Marshall. I hear you're pretty good. Do ya' play ball?"

"Yeah, I played football."

"Baseball, ya' play baseball? If this show goes through I want to put together a team. Everybody's gotta play."

"I played Little League ball," I answered.

"Were ya' good?"

"Yeah." I thought that he was asking weird questions for an acting role.

"Alright then, let's read."

I sat down and read with Millie. Again, I began incarnating my pal Howie. We finished, and Garry just sat there looking at me. Finally, "What position did ya' play?"

"First base," I said. It would be a year before I learned why he was asking so much about baseball.

"Call Tony and the group down," Garry told Millie before hurrying out. There was no, "Nice to meet ya'"— nothing.

Millie turned to me. "He likes you. Wait outside."

"What's goin' on?" I asked.

"He wants the network to approve you. Now, wait outside."

Totally confused, I walked back out again and sat down. Network? Approved? What the hell does that mean? I thought to myself. I sat there for close to an hour until a group of business-attired men and women quickly walked by me and into Millie's office. A moment later, Garry Marshall followed.

Again, Millie shut the door. All I could hear was muted conversation. Then the conversation stopped and the door opened. By now I knew my cue and immediately headed in. It turned out that the suited group was ABC Television executives. It was their job to approve Garry's choice for Potsie. They wanted to see me do my thing, so one last time I channeled Howie Shertzman. The execs actually laughed a few times. The moment I was done, Millie got up and thanked me for coming. Not you were good, bad, just thank you for coming.

What the hell! Thank you for coming? That's it? I didn't get the part? What a waste of my time. At least it stopped raining, I thought while walking back to my car.

By the time I arrived at my apartment, I had reevaluated the day. I'd decided that it was a good experience, regardless of the outcome. The phone was ringing as I walked in, but I'd had a long day, it was a long drive home, and I really needed to hit the head. As I was relieving myself, the ringing started again. I couldn't exactly answer so I let it go. Walking out of the bathroom, again the ringing. This time I picked it up. "Where the hell have you been?" screamed my agent.

"I just got back from the audition," I said.

"You got the part! Nine tomorrow morning, you need to be at the studio for wardrobe fittings and then rehearsal. You shoot the next day. A script with all the info is being couriered to you tonight."

Dumbfounded, all I could say was, "I got it?"

"Yes. Look, I gotta get your deal done. We'll talk later. Congrats!"

Numb, I stood there with the phone still in my hand.

The next morning, I found myself standing in the never-ending Paramount wardrobe department, a humongous warehouse of clothing history. It was here that I would meet Ron Howard, and I was a little in awe. *The Andy Griffith Show* was one of my favorites, and so was the movie, *The Music Man*. Ron had played the young boy with a lisp, Winthrop. He is the nicest and most generous person in the world, and on that initial day, when I was anxious, he immediately made me feel at ease and treated me like an equal. After we were finished in wardrobe, we headed for rehearsal and had immediate chemistry together.

Most people don't realize that there were two *Happy Days* pilots. The first one didn't have the characters of Fonzie or Ralph, and different actors were cast for the roles of Mr. Cunningham and Joanie, though Marion Ross still played Mrs. Cunningham. The tone was more like the movie *Summer of '42* and less like (the future) *American Graffiti*. It was an excellently reviewed pilot, and it aired on *Love, American Style* toward the end of 1972. Unfortunately, it didn't test well and was rejected by ABC as a series.

"Well, that's that." I said to myself when I learned we weren't picked up. I was certain I was going back to nodding parts. It felt so unfair. I thought about Willie and his insistence that "Some things supposed to be, make you go different ways; better ways to get dere."

I guess this wasn't the better way, Willie, I thought.

I've never been so wrong.

LESSON 4

Happy Days

"See mo' den whats you want to see."

So *Happy Days* didn't sell, but I landed a commercial agent and scored a part in the first singing McDonald's commercial. It was called "Clean Up Crew," and I worked with several actors, including John Amos (the father on the television series *Good Times*); we sang about the cleanliness of the restaurant. The spot is a classic because it introduced the jingle "You Deserve a Break Today"; Barry Manilow wrote the song itself.

Months passed. I continued getting roles, and both my acting skills and living conditions improved. I was able to afford the rent on a two-bedroom apartment with an extra half-bath, a sultan's fortress to me. Up till then, I had lived in places with only one bathroom, including my childhood home.

The parts I was offered also started improving: I landed a major role in the NBC Hallmark special, *Lisa, Bright and Dark*, based on the novel by John Neufeld, and starring Kay

Lenz, John Forsythe, and Anne Baxter. The story is about Lisa, a teenager who is succumbing to mental illness. Her sister, Kay, was played by Erin Moran, a young actress best known for the CBS series *Daktari* (about a veterinarian and his family). The Hallmark shoot was in San Francisco, and it was going terrifically. A few days before it wrapped, I received a call from my agent. "Guess what? ABC wants to do another *Happy Days* pilot."

American Graffiti had just been released. Ron Howard was in it, and the fifties were hot.

"Great!" I said, "When do we shoot?"

A moment of silence. "The network thinks that you and Ron might be too old. So before anything goes forward, they need to screen test the two of you together."

A longer moment of silence from my side. What the hell? "Okay," I responded, and hung up. "What the hell!" I said out loud. How could ABC make me screen test for a role that I already created? Okay, that Howie Shertzman created? Remember that old saying "He who owns the gold makes the rules?" It is 100 percent correct.

I arrived back in Los Angeles, and the next day went in for a *Happy Days* fitting. Again, Ron was there at the same time. When we were finished in wardrobe, a production assistant brought us the script for the screen test the following day. After looking it over Ron said to me, "I've done a bunch of screen tests and they never give anyone much time, so it's easy to come off stiff and uncomfortable. Let's find the stage we're shooting on and rehearse this. I think that we'll have a better shot."

It's no accident that he's so successful. Ron is smart now and he was smart then. "Makes sense," I answered.

We found the stage and rehearsed our scene, creating character bits that (we hoped!) would come off as spontaneous (and genius) at the shoot.

The next morning Garry Marshall was directing the screen tests, and fifteen duos were testing; each test was supposed to take twenty or so minutes. Garry spent two hours with us! He loved our "on the spot" creativity. Little did he know the hours Ron and I had spent to be on the spot.

A few days later, my agent called with the news that Howie Shertzman would live on! I got the part of Warren "Potsie" Weber (again). Hanging up the phone, I thought about the time that I complained to Willie about being second string and not playing enough in the football games, that the coach kept putting me in for only kick-offs, punts, etc. "You gots to see mo' den whats you want to see," he explained. Willie helped me see that my ability did not live up to my ego and fantasy. I honestly was not good enough to play first string, but the coach respected my commitment and hard work, and made sure that I earned a varsity letter by putting me in where he could. I didn't see the bigger picture; I only saw what I wanted to see. I would never make that same mistake again. I was disappointed when the first *Happy Days* pilot didn't get picked up. Now not only was it a better time to put the show on the air, but it also had the magic to stay on the air. There was a "better way to get there"!

Rehearsals started a few days after that phone call. I learned that Garry Marshall was still casting the role of Richie's younger sister, Joanie—they didn't want the girl from the original pilot. I told him that I had just worked with a terrific young actress on a Hallmark movie, *Lisa, Bright and Dark*, and that she'd be great for the part. He brought Erin Moran in for the callbacks, and she walked away with the role of Joanie Cunningham. Harold Gould, who had played Mr. Cunningham in the first pilot, was unavailable, so Tom Bosley was cast. Don Most had actually screen tested for Potsie (he was half of one of the fourteen other duos the network auditioned when they thought Ron and I might be too old) and they liked him so much they created the role of "Ralph Malph" just for him. One more minor character was added, and it turned out this one would make sure I was employed for the next ten and a half years. Arthur "Fonzie" Fonzarelli was not created to be a regular on the show. The casting came down to two actors: Micky Dolenz, famous from The Monkees, and a short, thin, unknown actor by the name of Henry Winkler.

I'll tell you a secret . . . Winkler got the part. Henry made the character his own, inventing the thumbs up, the magical knocks on the jukebox, the "not combing his hair because it was already perfect" move that was used during the opening credits, and the world-famous "Heyyyyy!"

Making this pilot was a blast. The entire cast bonded and got along great, and of course we all hoped that the show would take off this time. We didn't have to wait long; because of the success of *American Graffiti* and the Broadway musical *Grease*, ABC was quick to give us the pick-up, and wanted us on the air as soon as possible. When I got the news that the show was green-lighted, I thought back to that day when I almost went home without auditioning. And then I remembered how disappointed I was that the first pilot wasn't picked up. In both cases, Willie's advice encouraged me to move forward and keep trying. I am so grateful that I did. If I hadn't, I never would have experienced the most magical journey of my young life.

Two Pairs of Pants

*"Nobody mo' important cause things dey
own or job dey do."*

Happy Days premiered on January 15, 1974, just weeks after we wrapped the pilot. Things took off so fast that Garry and his staff could barely keep up with the writing: We were shooting only two shows ahead of what was airing. The pace was exhausting—we got up when it was dark and got home when it was dark. The sometimes 16-hour workdays on a dusty, old soundstage didn't leave time for anything else. We had no idea if the show was popular or not. My whole world became bed, shower, car, highway, shoot. And then reverse. One night I was talking with Willie in a dream just before waking up. "Nobody mo' important cause things dey own or job dey do. Good heart, dat's what make you mo' important," he said to me. It was strange; I'd been so busy I hadn't thought much about Willie (or anyone else outside of the cast) for a while.

★ ★ ★

As soon as we got ahead in our shooting and had some shows "in the can," the network put together the first *Happy Days* promotion tour: Henry, Don, Ron, and I were going to spend two weeks traveling to numerous states. Three of us would fly to Dallas together on a 6 a.m. flight; from there on, we would split up, Henry traveling with Don, and Ron (who had a commitment and couldn't fly to Dallas) with me. Then we would all meet again for an appearance on *The Mike Douglas Show* in Philadelphia.

We got our first taste of VIP service in Dallas. A very, very long, black, sparkling limo was waiting for us on the tarmac, right next to the plane. Henry, Don, and I felt like the fab three! The limo took us to a fancy hotel where we could quickly shower and get ready for our first appearance, an event at a park amphitheater. The network gave each of us suites with two bathrooms, and even a dining room—it was just crazy and kind of intimidating. I got ready quickly. It wasn't hard, as I'd only brought two pairs of pants, the ones that I was wearing, and one pair especially for *The Mike Douglas Show*, along with fourteen shirts and two weeks' worth of underwear and socks.

As I was leaving my suite, I noticed a housekeeper with a cleaning-supply cart knocking on a door next to mine. As it opened, a small boy ran out. The hallway was airy and fancy, but only had a low wall protecting you from falling ten stories to the lobby. The housekeeper went after the boy and she stopped him before he got to the wall. The kid began screaming for her to let him go just as his mother came out. I watched this richly-dressed young woman as she rudely grabbed her son, walked back to her room, placed the Do Not Disturb sign on the outside handle, and closed the door. She did not even say "thank you" to the person that might well have just saved her son's life.

Tears were in the housekeeper's eyes as I passed her on my way to the elevator. I could not believe what I had just witnessed. Was this how people with more than two pairs of pants to their name lived? Like they were better than the rest of us?

Back in the limo, Don, Henry, and I were excited about our first appearance together, but weren't certain anyone would show up. Since it was about a 45-minute drive to the event and none of us had eaten yet, an entire meal of sandwiches, salads, and drinks was set up in the car on a pop-up table. I felt like we had definitely landed in The Twilight Zone.

We knew the amphitheater was located in a large park. As we were driving up to it, we saw a huge crowd a few hundred yards away, and figured that a big concert must be going on. That was sort of strange, we agreed, because it was the middle of the afternoon. Driving up closer, the screams started. They were there for us! At that moment, our lives changed forever. A few weeks before, we were just regular guys fighting to get dates like everyone else. Now we felt like the hottest guys in the country, as hordes of girls literally began sprinting toward our limo. I think the only force more powerful than an atom bomb is an emotionally charged teen girl: They started rocking the limo, and the police had to physically drag them off. It was absolutely surreal.

Finally, with a line of police on both sides, we were rushed out of the limo and almost carried into the back of the theater. It felt like we were doing a remake of The Beatles' *A Hard Day's Night*; that, or a Fellini movie. None of us had ever experienced anything like it before. And we had no idea that it was only a short preview of what was to happen to each of us on a regular basis.

The police slammed the theater door shut, and all was silent within—that was as disconcerting as the pandemonium outside. The theater staff put wireless mikes on each of us. It turned out that the event was a women's fashion show, and that we were to go on stage to speak with the audience, the largest crowd in the amphitheater's history. We got the cue to go. Walking out, we could feel the energy of over thirty thousand women who had attended just to get a glimpse of us. As soon as the audience caught sight of us, the screaming rose to a furious pitch. Lines of police were down front to protect us from girls rushing the stage. The three of us just stood there, dumbfounded, not really knowing what to do. Finally, Henry did a double thumbs up, "Heyyyyyy!"

That place exploded into decibels that reached fainting levels. Taking it all in, I turned to Henry and said, "I think we're going to get lucky."

Soon, we were back in the limo and returning to the hotel. The police had taken us out a different way to avoid the screaming throng. All of us were absolutely numb from the experience; we knew that life adjustments would be coming fast and furious. Henry had the best line, "And I thought that my bar mitzvah was exciting."

Personally, I wasn't sure if what we had just lived through was exciting or terrifying. But yes, it was definitely better than my own bar mitzvah.

When we got back to the hotel, we all went to our rooms to rest before dinner. I found the door to my suite ajar. I stepped in to my room and a thirteen-year-old girl with braces accosted me. "I love you!" she screamed.

Startled, I didn't know what to say. She grabbed me in a hug that was stronger than the Jaws of Life. Gently prying her off, I said, "You have to go."

"No!" she responded, and went in for another monster hug.

Side-stepping her, I said, "You can't be in here."

Looking around, she said, "Do you have a picture?"

"I don't, but if you give me your address I'll send you one."

"No!" she screamed. "I'll only leave if I have something to prove that I met you in person!"

I noticed the monogrammed hotel towels. "What if I give you a towel?"

This seemed to pique her interest. "One from your bathroom?"

"Absolutely," I replied.

She mulled this over for a moment and then said, "Only if you used it."

"I did."

"You have to sign it." Pulling out a red Sharpie from her pocket, she insisted, "Has to be in red."

"Deal," I replied.

I grabbed a damp towel from the open bathroom, and signed my very first autograph, one that I'd never forget. The girl grabbed it, gave me one more rib-crushing hug, and rushed out. I rested and then freshened up for dinner. I kept thinking, "I am a household name. Wow!"

I left my room to meet the others for dinner, feeling important. As I walked down the hallway, I noticed the same housekeeper who had helped the young boy earlier. She was having trouble getting supplies from her cart, so I stopped to help. She gave me the most genuine, beautiful smile, before getting back to work. It became so clear to me that, between us, she was the real star and, equally important, she was an unselfish, giving person who cared about others first. And then I thought of that dream I had about Willie. "Nobody mo' important cause things dey own or job dey do. Good heart, dat's what make you mo' important." I made up my mind, then and there, that no matter how strange being famous became, I would always be as generous and giving to others as possible. Even when they wanted me to sign dirty towels.

In case you were wondering, by the time I got to Philly, my pants were standing up by themselves. I threw them away, and wore *The Mike Douglas Show* pair home.

LESSON 6

Singing to a Bulldog

"You gotta gift, gotta use it right."

My entrepreneurial adventures started at the age of nine. My dad had created original cartoon characters on stationery while he was in college. He never did anything with them though, and a large, dusty box sat stored in our small garage. Every night at home, all I ever heard was my parents arguing about money. We didn't have much and my mom wouldn't work. She felt that she needed to be at home with me. I felt that she needed to go to work; felt it, didn't say it.

One summer morning, as I was getting my bike from the garage, I noticed the grubby box and, Bam! It all came together. I would take my dad's cartoon stationery and sell it door-to-door! I would "make money" and "make everything fine." I told my mom that I was going to my friend Jeff Schredder's house—he lived two doors down. Instead, I cleaned up that box of "Looney Letters" and I loaded it on my old wagon. That night at dinner, I proudly placed over ten dollars on the table. When asked where I got it, I told them the story. I actually thought I saw a hint of pride in my parents' faces, even though they said to never, ever do that again. The money didn't stop my parents' arguments, but it did make me realize that I had a talent for knowing how to sell things.

Years later, while working with Willie, I was helping to take refrigerators with freezer compartments out of their shipping boxes so that they could be brought onto the appliance sales floor. All of the brochures we unpacked stated that new technology prevented ice from forming on the sides of the freezer compartment. I said to Willie, "They should have a big, red sign that says 'Freezes Food, Not Your Freezer.' Bet they'd sell a bunch more."

Willie stopped working and stared at me.

"What?" I said.

"You right! Dat is smart, boy."

I felt a surge of pleasure. "Not a big deal," I replied.

"Is a big deal! You gotta' gift of knowin' words dat make people buy things, gotta use it right, boy." He put his hand on my shoulder, looked me in the eye and repeated, "Gotta use it right." After he was sure it registered, he went off to speak with the appliance manager. Two days later, a banner soared above the appliance area. It stated in red: "Freeze Your Food, Not Your Freezer." Fifteen years old, and I felt like an official marketer. Leonard's sold a bunch of those refrigerators.

I really believe that those marketing skills helped me move forward in show biz. They definitely helped on *Happy Days*. In the seventies, we weren't paid like today's television stars; salaries were decent, but not extravagant. I innately knew that

I could supplement my income by using the show for other opportunities. But what could I market? After watching a re-run of *The Partridge Family*, I had the answer. The fifties were known for cars, girls, and music. *Happy Days* had everything except a band. Maybe my talent night skills could pay off . . .

The next day, I spoke with Garry Marshall. He was busy and didn't have much time, so I did a quick, elevator market-ing pitch: "We have girls, we have cars, where's the music? What if Potsie sings in a band?"

He thought for a moment and then said, "A band would be good. Ralph and Richie could also be in it. You sing good?"

"Yeah, pretty good," I replied.

"Alright, but you gotta pick a song."

Yes!

Starting to leave, he added, "I'll have ya' sing to a bulldog. If you're not good, I'll get laughs, and if you're good, I'll still get laughs." And then he left.

That's how I sold my first televised singing gig—the right words at just the right time. I also acquired some respon-sibility beyond acting: choosing a song and recording it. I remembered that Willie was a huge fan of Elvis Presley, so, in his honor, I picked one of Elvis's most famous songs, "All Shook Up." There was a frat party scene in the next epi-sode of *Happy Days*, and that's where Garry wrote in the new band. And yes, I sang to a bulldog. Garry liked it, and started adding the band to about every third episode.

From this, I was able to get a record deal (on the same label as David Cassidy), put together my own (real life) band, and book concerts all over country. By using my talent, I was able to create a whole other business for myself beyond

Happy Days. I was in charge of all the band's music on the show, and was fortunate enough to write some originals with my composing partner, Ron Rose. These experiences really benefited my future producing endeavors. Perhaps best of all, Garry was proud of me. He said that instead of complaining about the size of my salary, I used what I had to create more opportunity for myself. Whenever I look back on those days, I do so acknowledging two things: Without Garry, I would never have had the option to move my career in the directions that I have, and without Willie, I never would have realized that I had gifts beyond acting to share.

Day With a Beatle

"Da real great people is humble."

Despite the craziness in Texas, *Happy Days* was only a modest hit as we came to the end of the first season (we didn't become a phenomenon, and the number one show in the world, until the third season). Still, Fonzie, Richie, Ralph, and Potsie were hugely popular. Of course, viewers only knew the characters we played; as guys we were all basically nerds, and we knew we were only "hot" because we were on the tube. I won't lie though: We all took full advantage of our new status with the ladies—all of us except Ron. He was in love with his high school sweetheart, Cheryl. She was the love of his life and the girl he married.

Actually, Ron was the main reason we all stayed pretty normal. He was the seasoned pro in the group, and already famous when we started. His work ethic, lack of ego, and great character influenced all of us to follow suit. He was the leader and set the tone for everybody. Henry Winkler, Don Most, and I owe him a great debt of gratitude.

One day during lunch break, Ron told me he wanted me to meet somebody, but he wouldn't say whom. It turned out it was John Wayne. He was shooting a promotional spot near us. Ron had worked with him on his last movie, *The Shootist*. When John Wayne spotted Ron, he instantly left the set and gave him a bear hug. Ron introduced me, and I'll never forget John Wayne's words: "Nice meeting you, Anson. You stick with Ron here and you might have a chance of staying in this business. He's going to go far."

Well, he couldn't have been more right.

Another time, I complained to Ron about everyone calling me Potsie.

"What are you complaining about?" he said. "I'm stuck with two, Opie and Richie."

I had to laugh. Then he put it all into perspective. "Of course people are going to call us by our characters' names; that's how they know us. We have to earn our real names. We need to accomplish things as individuals."

His words were a Ph.D. in moving forward and never resting on your laurels.

One early morning, we were shooting some simple scenes on a smaller stage. Ron, Henry, Don, a guest star, and I were the only ones working. During a lighting set up I walked over to what looked like a large tin can of coffee. Craft service (which today provides gourmet snacks, lattes, and organic pies) was not a big deal back then. Stale coffee and old apples were pretty much it. In fact, Louie, our set electrician and bookie, was in charge of it. You were lucky to get milk with the black sludge. Anyway, while I was pouring a cup I noticed a man who looked just like John Lennon with a young boy. Walking back, I told Ron and Don.

"Yeah, right," Don said. "John Lennon wants to hang out with us."

It turned out it was John Lennon! He was with his ten-year-old son, Julian, and they did want to hang out with us! John was out in Los Angeles, and his son's favorite show was *Happy Days*. They had come to the set totally unannounced to meet us. John was a huge fan of the fifties and said he also loved the show. I was speechless, but John turned out to be a real down-to-earth genius. He was kind and so damn funny. He said that Elvis Presley was a major influence on his music, and that Elvis was "everlasting." Soon, we all felt like we'd known each other forever. When he told me that he liked my singing, I was floored. One of the greatest talents of all time actually heard me sing? Ahhhhhhhhh!

John and Julian spent the entire day on the set, twelve hours, all the way to wrap. John was truly humble; he seemed to radiate light. Watching how he treated everyone on the set made me think of something Willie told me. "Da real great people is humble cause dey know dat dey God's angels." John drew ink caricatures for most of the crew but not for the cast. We were professionals and didn't want to bother him by asking for one . . . Dumb! Today I bet crew members paid off their houses with their original Lennon doodles. I do have one remembrance of that magical day: We all took a photo with John and Julian that sits on my desk. I experienced greatness that day. None of us would ever see him again, but his light, the light of greatness, continues to shine.

"Da real great people is humble cause dey know dat dey God's angels."

Three-Camera Magic

"Gotta drop to da bottom to find da way."

"Dey times things need to be so bad to be so good." Willie told me this when I got caught cheating on a math test. "Gotta drop to da bottom to find da way." My parents made my life hell, but it changed my study habits around and I never cheated again.

It turns out changes were happening in the *Happy Days* camp. We had dropped to 48th place in the ratings by the end of the second season. It was looking like we might not get picked up. Then ABC hired a brilliant programmer, Fred Silverman, as its new president. He believed that, possibly, there was still hope for the show. He convinced Garry Marshall to make Fonzie the major character, and Garry convinced Fred to change *Happy Days* to a three-camera show with a live audience. He felt that the cast was good enough to handle it, and that the show would be funnier.

There was one big hurdle: Garry hadn't yet spoken to

Ron about taking a back seat to "the Fonz," and, contractu-ally, Ron had to approve it. Ron had no qualms about tak-ing a back seat; this is what made Ron so unique. In a crazy business, he never let ego interfere with what was best for the show. At a young age, he had the character and insight of a sage. I suggested to Garry that the cast use all of its resources to bring viewers back to the show: We should do television and radio interviews, newspaper stories, whatever we could get to keep the show in the public eye. We did and it worked. We went up slightly in the ratings and secured the pick-up for season three.

Stage 19 became our new home, and we had the same camera crew as *The Lucy Show*. (Coincidentally, *The Lucy Show* had shot on the same stage. One of the show's original crew members said to me that Lucy squeezed a good luck charm her mother had given her when she was a child into a crack located in one of the stage's walls. Rumor has it that it's still there, bringing luck to all who film on that stage.)

★ ★ ★

I'll never forget the excitement of our first live show. We were all backstage and could feel the audience's energy as they were taken to their grandstand-type seats. Tom, Mar-ion, Don, Henry, and I all had stage experience and loved the thrill of going live. But Ron had never acted in front of an audience, and he was visibly nervous. About ten minutes before our director, Jerry Paris, made cast introductions, I looked around and didn't see Ron anywhere. Then I checked the wardrobe room and saw him, a man alone, standing by some racks. He noticed me and then turned away without saying a word. Clearly he was scared. He stole a few more quiet moments before he took a deep breath, and then walked toward the group, giving me a nervous smile and nod as he passed, ready to face his greatest fear.

It turned out he had nothing to worry about: Ron was terrific and so was the entire cast. It was a magical evening, and at the end of the show the entire studio audience was on their feet, cheering and applauding. The new format and the magic it created had the same effect on the television audience at home, and in a few short months *Happy Days* became the number one television show in the world. We enjoyed record-breaking ratings, and it was because of *Happy Days* that ABC became the number one network for the first time in its history.

Willie was right, we had to fail to find our way and win. "Dey times things need to be so bad to be so good. Gotta drop to da bottom to find da way."

We were on that stage for a long time, and I looked for Lucy's lucky charm for years. I thought I saw something twinkle once while we were shooting, but then couldn't find it again. I don't think that we're supposed to . . . it gave us the luck to move forward.

Playing Ball

"Da game take me away."

The only bigger fan of the Los Angeles Dodgers than me was Willie. I'd spent my childhood rooting for them in the cheapest seats. So imagine what a high it was for me when I learned that the *Happy Days* softball team would play charity games in every major stadium in the United States. Our opponents would be professional football, hockey, or basketball teams—and occasionally, the casts of other television shows.

"Baseball, ya' play baseball?" What I didn't know at the time of my first audition for the role of Potsie: Garry Marshall was a special boss. I thought he was asking weird questions for an acting role, but he wasn't. He had a plan. Not only did he want to help nurture his cast's creative possibilities, such as acting, writing, producing, and directing, to ensure that everyone he hired would have a chance at a long-term career in the volatile world of show biz; he also wanted to inspire us to be better people. This was the reason that he insisted we have a *Happy Days* softball team. He believed that traveling together as a team would have a positive effect on the show, since it was hard to be petty on set with a teammate who had sacrificed a hit so that you could score and win the game.

When we played in Dodger Stadium, I could not believe I was actually standing on the field, mingling with my heroes. Willie told me he would spend hours on the bus just to see a game. He'd say to me, "Da game take me away. Whiles I sit dere and watch, everythin's possible. It my damn Green Cathedral."

And here I was, playing a game in the stadium! If only Willie was still on this earth. I wanted him to be there. I could have taken him down to the green grass of his church. It was an incredible thrill to hear a full stadium roaring their approval as I ran the bases, my image fifty feet high on the video scoreboard. I wanted him to experience that and I wanted him hear me sing: I had the privilege of singing the "Star-Spangled Banner" before each main game, an honor that I'll always cherish.

One Saturday morning, after we'd played many charity games around the country, I received a call from a family friend. The commanding general of the U.S. Third Infantry Division in Germany wanted to know if we would fly over and play a series of games with his troops. He promised he would make sure that we had a great experience. I brought it up to Garry and the cast, and everyone wanted to go. The dates were planned and soon we were all in the air, beer and schnapps in hand, toasting our way to Frankfurt.

We were all put up in an adorable gasthaus about an hour south of Frankfurt, in a town called Würzburg, on the Rhine

River. Würzburg is over a thousand years old and still has the character and charm of a Grimm's fairytale. Gasthauses are a mainstay throughout Germany, a quaint motel-type accommodation with a restaurant.

The first night the general and his staff hosted a dinner for us in a restaurant created in a thousand-year-old castle that overlooked the entire city and the Rhine River. It still had its original stone walls and floors, authentic suits of armor, swords, and other weapons. Instead of water on the table, there were white and red wine dispensers. We could place our glass under either one and "fill 'er up."

It was a "Happy" night to say the least.

After dinner Ron, Henry, Don, and I explored the historic fortress, ending up outside on a large balcony that overlooked the silent, twinkling city below. The only sound was the moving water of the Rhine. There we were, four ordinary young guys, sharing an unforgettable experience. Ron started quietly singing the words, "Splish splash I was taking a bath," and soon we were all singing, four real friends, together, belting out Bobby Darren to a sleepy German village. It was a moment in time that I knew I'd treasure my entire life.

We played five games against army troops of the Third Division based in different areas, and it became apparent that what we were really doing was much more important than playing games. We were the spirit of the United States to soldiers and their families who had been stationed in Germany for a long time and needed a shot of home, a few hours to escape to better times. At the end of the final game, an African American private walked up to me for an autograph and said, "I've been overseas for three years and before watching you guys play today, I was in a real funk. You got me out of it and I can't thank you enough for that." He gave me a hug and walked on.

Years later, I was honored to represent small businesses at the first U.S. Trademark Exposition held at the headquarters of the U.S. Patent and Trademark Office in Alexandria, Virginia. My business partner, JoAnna Connell, and I had created a company called StarMaker Products. After the opening ceremony and all of the speeches, a well-dressed man came up to me and said, "I don't know if you remember, but when I was in the army, I met you in Germany at a *Happy Days* game. I want you to know how much you helped me that day. That was the start of getting out of a really bad place in my head."

It turned out that the young private was now a prominent patent attorney. He gave me another hug and walked away, with the head of the entire U.S. Patent Office.

"Da game take me away. While I sit dere and watch, everythin's possible. It's my damn Green Cathedral." No more cheap seats, Willie. You were on that field with us running the bases, making 'everythin's' possible; giving hope and the American spirit to all who watched.

All Shook Up

"God talk thru dat boy. He gots da gift. He be forever."

Leonard's had a "Fifties Sale," when I worked there as an assistant janitor. All furniture was marked down to a price that would have been charged in the 1950s, and period-appropriate music blared out of the store's speakers. Whenever Elvis came on, Willie would start dancing while he was mopping, and I watched as hard years fell away from his face. "God talk thru dat boy," he'd say with reverence. "He gots da gift. He be forever."

I loved watching Willie look and play like a kid, never dreaming that I'd meet his idol, Elvis Presley.

Right at the start of *Happy Days*, I committed to doing cerebral palsy telethons around the country. I had a personal interest: My cousin, Annie, was born with cerebral palsy (CP). My aunt and uncle were amazing, selfless parents, but they struggled with the heavy financial burden of her care. It felt good to turn the popularity of the show into dollars for United

Cerebral Palsy (a charity that truly cares; ninety percent of all monies donated go directly to those in need). In early May of 1975, one of the bookings was a telethon in Monroe, Louisiana. It didn't sound like the most thrilling place to travel, but off I went. I was picked up at the airport by a hard-working single mom, Katie, and her ten-year-old son, Bobby, who had a moderate case of CP. Katie and Bobby's dad had set a date to be married, but when Katie had an amniocentesis done and found out that their baby would be born disabled, her groom-to-be vanished, never to be heard from again. Katie had her baby and took on the mammoth responsibility of raising him alone. She told me she was the district manager of a national food franchise that consisted of eighty-nine stores—quite a major accomplishment for a single mom without a degree. She had convinced corporate to be one of the sponsors for the telethon, and then volunteered to help. Bobby was a huge fan of *Happy Days*, and he asked me to sing a song. All three of us sang "All Shook Up" until we reached my hotel.

Looking back, it was prophetic.

The telethon would be live from Saturday at noon until 6 p.m. Sunday: thirty hours of live broadcast. Katie told me that my pick-up for rehearsal was at 10 a.m. Bobby asked me for a hug before they left, and I could feel the overwhelming love inside of this child.

As I walked into the lobby of the hotel, I noticed a local paper with an ad for an Elvis Presley concert on Saturday night at the Monroe Civic Auditorium. That turned out to be right across the parking lot from the building that would be airing the telethon. After singing "All Shook Up" in Katie's car, this felt like more than a simple coincidence.

On Saturday, rehearsal went well and the show was going great, taking in record contributions. There was a surprise call from Elvis's representative, donating a generous $5,000 from the superstar. I learned about it in the green room, a place for performers to rest and get some food, and wondered if Elvis was actually watching the show. Katie and her son popped in. She had just finished work (she worked weekends, too) and Bobby wanted to say, "Hi." We talked about the success of the telethon and made small talk, and then I mentioned the Elvis concert I'd read about, that was happening a few hundred yards away.

Katie asked, "Would you like to meet him?"

"Huh?" I answered, a worldly response.

It turned out, a friend of Elvis's named Red had come into a local restaurant where she and her son were eating and they struck up a conversation. Red connected with Bobby, and gave Katie a number to call if they wanted to see the concert and meet Elvis. Katie asked me again, "Do you want to meet Elvis?"

"Sure," I said, not believing that it was possible.

Hours later, I had just finished singing "Splish Splash" when Katie rushed up to me backstage. "Elvis finished his concert and wants to meet you."

Again, my worldly response, "Huh?"

"Red says that Elvis will be taking pictures and then going straight to his car through the backstage door."

Within moments, Katie, Bobby and I were heading across the enormous parking lot to the Civic Center. We reached the stage door and sure enough, parked right outside was a 1975 Lincoln limo. Katie talked to the security men and after a few walkie-talkie conversations, we were allowed to move Bobby's wheelchair right next to the car. The three of us waited, and then the stage door opened and out walked a sequined Elvis, followed by his entourage.

"Where's Bobby?" he asked.

He looked heavier than his golden days, but he still had tremendous charisma and something more, just like Willie had said years before. Elvis took off his scarf and tied it around Bobby's neck. I could tell that he was a man with a kind and caring heart. He spent a few minutes talking with Bobby, and he made that little boy feel like a superstar. Then he walked over to me, put both hands on my shoulders, and said, "Very nice to meet you, Anson. I really like your show."

Huh? This time I caught myself and said, "Thanks." I was in total awe.

"I was in my room before the show and watched you on the telethon. You sing darn good."

Oh my God, Oh my God, Oh my God! Elvis saw me sing! "I'm just okay," I said.

"No, you got something special."

I instantly flashed back to when I first met Willie. I told Elvis about him, how he had said those same words to me when I was fifteen years old, and how much he had meant to me. I also told him how Willie had idolized him.

"You know, I had someone like that in my life," Elvis said and it looked like he was tearing up. "As soon as I graduated high school, I got a job on a factory line to help my family out. Working next to me was an older man named Frank. I was a young guy without a lot of confidence who wanted to sing, but I had no idea how a poor kid like me would even get a chance. I could have given up and become an electrician or something, but he heard me sing while working the line, and convinced me to stick with it, said that it would all work out. If it weren't for him, I don't think that I would be here today."

I stood there, next to The King, stunned silent. One of Elvis's entourage signaled that they had to go.

"It was nice talking with you, Anson. I hope we have a chance to do it again."

Elvis started to shake my hand, but I spontaneously hugged him. Laughing, he walked over to Bobby, bent down, and gave him a bear hug before getting into his limo.

Katie, Bobby, and I watched as the limo drove off into the silent night, touched by his genuine kindness. I would never see him again, and Elvis died two years later, but like Willie and John Lennon said, his gift is everlasting.

Kidnapped by the President's Daughter

"You listen, boy. In people's heads, dey makes people bigger and better den dey are. Peoples dey never even met. Dey got to earn yer respect."

It was a frigid and rain-soaked Saturday afternoon. Willie and I were both married to our wide-aisle mops, cleaning the mud that was being generously dispersed by soggy customers. On this dreary day, Fred Ames, the owner of Leonard's Department Store, decided to have his wife and daughter visit him at work. Fred was all over us, making sure that the store would be sparkling clean for their arrival, a definite challenge given the horrible weather. I was nervous about meeting Fred's daughter. I'd seen pictures of her on his desk and I could see that she was beautiful and way out of my social level. I said as much to Willie.

"You listen, boy. In people's heads, dey makes people bigger and better den dey are. Peoples dey never even met. Dey got to earn yer respect. You just as big, boy. You remember dat."

Fred's family showed up during our lunch break. His wife was aloof, not friendly to anybody, and his daughter, who was even more beautiful than her pictures, hardly looked at me when we were introduced. Suddenly, she wasn't so beautiful. I thought about what Willie said to me. Who the hell was she to try and make me feel small? What had she done to make her special? She was a spoiled brat. I pushed her out of my head and placed her into my mental dumpster. Then I went back to work.

What's interesting was that something noticeably changed in me after I did this, because soon she actually looked around and found me cleaning up the appliance section and tried to be nice. Was it a classic case of "you want what you can't have"? I can tell you it was pretty clear that she definitely wasn't used to a janitor who couldn't care less about her. I saw her much differently after thinking over what Willie had said, and I showed her that I had better things to do with my time than talk to the boss's daughter . . . like wiping off refrigerators. "You just as big, boy. You remember dat."

★ ★ ★

Singing on *Happy Days* opened up many great opportunities for me. One in particular started with a phone call from my agent. Susan Ford, the President's daughter, was being crowned queen of the International Azalea Festival in Norfolk, Virginia. She had requested that I sing "America the Beautiful" at her coronation. Blown away, I said, "Yeah!"

This would be so much better than singing to a bulldog!

I arrived in Norfolk, Virginia, and was immediately whisked away to an orchestra rehearsal at the event location—

a magnificent ballroom in one of the finer area hotels. Everyone involved was terrific and the rehearsal went perfectly. On my way out, one of the volunteers asked if I'd like to meet the President's daughter. She had just finished a final fitting for her gown.

"Absolutely," I said. "She's the reason I'm here."

We walked into an adjoining room, and there was Susan Ford, looking beautiful, talking with a couple of girlfriends. We were introduced, and all she said was "Hi" before turning back to her friends. Her tone was cold and curt.

Instantly, I flashed back to the day that I met Fred's daughter. President's daughter or not, Susan Ford didn't earn my respect. So without uttering a word, I turned and walked out. Tracking down the chairman, I said, in no uncertain terms, that if he wanted me to attend the event and sing, he'd have to change the seating arrangements. There was no way that I'd be sitting in close proximity to Susan Ford.

After some considerable arguing, he finally agreed.

The event was spectacular, black-tie elegant. After the coronation, I sang, and then the room full of dignitaries was seated for dinner. I was sitting at least five tables away from Susan Ford, and I avoided eye contact with her all evening. The orchestra played through dinner and then, before dessert, a few couples got up to dance. I felt a tap on my shoulder.

"Would you please dance with me?" It was Susan. "These people are driving me nuts."

She appeared to be sincere so I said, "Sure."

"I'm really sorry that I was so rude to you," she whispered. "Something happened and I was upset. Didn't mean to take it out on you."

She earned my respect in that moment by being straight up and honest.

It turned out that Susan Ford had a great personality and was a lot of fun; we became inseparable for the rest of the evening. After taking a walk around the pristine hotel grounds (followed closely by the secret service) I said goodnight at the front door of her suite. We shared a tender kiss, and I departed. I wasn't thinking, "I just kissed the President of the United States' daughter." I was thinking about a girl who I felt was really great.

I went back home, and back to work. An official invitation from the White House arrived in the mail. An afternoon tea reception was being hosted by Betty Ford and her daughter, Susan, to thank the executive committee of the Azalea Festival. Interesting, I thought. Especially because I was never on any committee . . .

I was working the day before the event, and had to fly a red-eye to Washington. It was a turbulent flight. After we landed I was driven to a nice Embassy Suites, where I slept a few hours before it was time to get ready. Still a bit out of sorts from the rough flight and a lack of sleep, I was picked up and driven to the White House.

After checking in I was escorted—with other festival folks—to the famous East Room. Waiting for us were tuxedoed helpers offering delicious iced tea and tiny sandwiches. After a few minutes, we were asked to form a receiving line. Looking up, I saw the First Lady and Susan glide down a beautiful staircase. Then they walked down the line to thank each person individually.

Reaching me, Betty Ford greeted me by name, shared

how much Susan had liked my singing, and mentioned how nice I was to her. I couldn't believe that the First Lady even knew my name. Susan then walked up with mischief in her eyes.

"Nice place ya' got here," I said.

"Well, you'll just have to see more of it," she responded before moving on.

Both Susan and her mother departed soon after thanking the final guest. One of the White House staff announced that the First Lady had granted all of us a special VIP tour of the White House that would include Lincoln's Bedroom. The tour was long, and I was so exhausted by the time we reached that bedroom that I had to sit in a chair as the guide spoke about its history. All I could think about was my hotel bed and sleep. Then I felt a tap on my shoulder. A Secret Service agent said, "Susan would like to see you. Please follow me, sir."

Bam! My adrenaline kicked in and instantaneously I was wide awake.

I followed him to the elevator that takes you up to the family residence. A kind, older gentleman was at the controls. He said he'd been working that elevator for thirty-five years. He took us up to the third floor. Then the agent and I walked down a short corridor. Stopping, the Secret Service guy pointed to a room. "Susan's inside, sir."

He left and I walked into the famous solarium! Built by President Taft, it was the same room where President Nixon told his family that he was resigning. It had been turned into a hangout for the Ford kids. Susan ran up to me and gave me a beer. "Told you you'd see more of this place."

I thought she looked great in jeans and a T-shirt. A few

of her girlfriends were there with her. The solarium has huge windows overlooking the expansive White House lawn. I could see Liberty, the President's golden retriever, running around, and tourists looking through the fence. I had a sudden urge to call my best friend, Jeff Schredder, and let him guess where I was. This was 1975, though, and cell phones were not invented yet, never mind texting. All we had were answering machines, and Jeff didn't even have that convenience. I called him from a landline but his phone just kept ringing and ringing. Jeff never did answer his first (and only) call from the White House residence.

Susan's friends were nice and we had a great time hanging out and talking. I was feeling tired again, so I told Susan that I'd need to be getting back to my hotel.

"No way," she said. "I'm kidnapping you to a Harold Melvin and the Blue Notes concert."

Again, I was jolted awake. I freshened up in her bathroom, where I was gifted with a brand new White House toothbrush and used some of her personal toothpaste. I was a bit surprised at the lack of luxuries in the personal residence. Her bedroom appeared a little old-fashioned, and the aged bathroom had basic Holiday Inn type towels. Even the redone solarium had antiquated, lived-in furniture and a small, outdated kitchen. Not everything was as grand as I'd imagined it, but when we left the White House—talk about intimidating! Susan and I were seated in an official limousine, while numerous other black vehicles were positioned in front of and behind us, all filled with agents.

Driving through Washington on a date with the President's daughter was simply unreal. When we reached the venue, Susan and I were separated and taken to different entrances. We met again at our seats.

The concert was great. When it ended, Susan suggested that we get something to eat. To this day, I don't know what possessed me to do this, but I insisted that I pay. I had only $5 in my pocket. So the President's daughter, the entire Secret Service detail and I got in line at Roy Rogers Roast Beef in Georgetown. Susan was a great sport about it and our bill came in just under my limit. Famished, we downed the sandwiches and fries.

At the end of the night the entire entourage drove to my hotel. Susan walked with me, alone, to the entrance. I told her it was a magical night. She gave me a warm hug and a kiss that I'll never forget. She then turned and walked back to the open door of the waiting limo. Watching the caravan drive off, I wasn't sleepy anymore; in fact, I'd never felt more alive.

Uncle Hank's Heimlich Maneuver

"You give back, dat's how it's 'posed to be."

My responsibilities as an assistant janitor went beyond cleaning. One Saturday afternoon, Willie and I were delivering a dining room set to a large home in an upscale Burbank neighborhood. The lady of the household met us at the door and graciously showed us where to set up her new furniture. Carrying everything inside, we noticed a children's party going on in the expansive backyard. It turned out that she and her husband had adopted disabled twins. They had welcomed the pair into their family at three years of age; this was their seventh birthday. The couple also had two biological teenagers, and they were supervising the fun along with their mom and dad. The family's love, patience, and connection with each other were awe-inspiring to me. It was obvious that their considerable earthly goods had not corrupted their large hearts. Watching the children from the dining room window, tears started running down Willie's cheeks.

"What's wrong?" I asked. I'd never seen him upset like that.

Wiping his tears he said, "I had an older sister dat was born like dose kids . . . name was Maggie . . . loved her so much." He broke down, not able to control his sobbing. "One day I gets home and she gone. My mom cryin' hard, my dad sayin' couldn't afford her no mo'. Never saw her again." He took a step closer to me. "You promise me, boy, you promise dat you gonna help people. You gonna be able to do dat. Like dey rich people here, you give back, dat's how it's 'posed to be . . . you always give back, boy, so nobody lose der family."

We all experience moments in life that can define us if we allow them to, and that moment with Willie was mine. I promised him that I would always give back. I was a kid, but I instinctively knew that he didn't just mean money; he was asking me to be aware of others. He was asking me to step outside of myself so that I could help people in their moment of need—from opening a door, to saving a life—whatever that moment of connection called out for. I promised him that I would always give back. I meant it, and it turned out that Willie's wisdom saved many lives.

The same year that *Happy Days* premiered, the Heimlich maneuver was gaining regional attention. Dr. Henry Heimlich is my uncle—actually second cousin, but we are close, and I've always called him Uncle Hank. He created things to improve people's lives, and invented new medical devices—the Heimlich Chest Valve, the Micro Trach, and a portable iron lung (created with Neil Armstrong, yes, the first man on the moon)— in addition to the Heimlich maneuver. When we visited each other, we would have long discussions about the importance of alternative medicine. His wife, Jane Murray Heimlich (daughter of Arthur and Kathryn Murray of ballroom dance acclaim), authored *What Your Doctor Doesn't Tell You*. A pioneer in alternative therapy, she had a huge influence on Uncle Hank. She convinced him that there are effective ways to achieve better long-term health without unwarranted, expensive prescription drugs and surgical procedures recommended by profit-driven companies and individuals. She had long insisted that drug companies, food manufacturers, chemical companies, and uninformed doctors were causing unnecessary illnesses, and that unless the American people took charge of their own health, ate the right foods, exercised regularly, and stopped depending on quick-fix pills, our entire health care system would fail. Jane was right, and today our system is in a crisis mode.

My uncle looked beyond quick fixes: He researched the history of a disease, examined past cures, and then invented a more natural way to proceed that wouldn't cause the patient more problems. His results were impressive, but were challenged by large pharmaceutical and chemical companies, as well as the highly influential American Red Cross and the Food and Drug Administration (FDA), both of which were subject to intense lobbying by these companies. Why? Because Uncle Hank was threatening the companies' bottom lines and stock values. Today, even at ninety-two years old, Hank refuses to back down. He is constantly confronting the demons he perceives behind our country's broken health care system.

Not long after the band became a regular part of *Happy Days*, my Uncle Hank flew out to Los Angeles for meetings that would educate people about the importance and effectiveness of the Heimlich maneuver. He stopped by the set to visit me, and he complained about how hard it was to bring serious attention to the maneuver. As incredible as it may seem now, at the time the Red Cross was a major hurdle; they insisted that a slap on the back was the correct method to dislodge food in a choking victim and made sure that this was the message the media conveyed.

As Hank and I chatted, I received a set call from *The Merv Griffin Show*. I had appeared on the show a few weeks earlier, and they told me they'd ask me back. Now they were in a bit of a bind—someone had dropped out at the last minute and they wanted to know if I'd be available again that night. I looked over at Hank, and Willie's words echoed back, "You give back, boy, so nobody lose der family." Instantly, everything connected and I hatched a plan.

I said that I'd do the show, but first I made sure that Hank was available, and that he could meet me there. I hurried home to shower and grab the charts of the song that I'd be singing on the program. Hank met me at the theater, and was then seated in the audience. I looked all over for Merv, but he was busy, and then the show started and I still hadn't had a chance to speak with him about what I wanted to do for my uncle. I was running out of time—and then the magic happened. After I sang my tune there was a commercial break and I was moved over to the panel to be interviewed by Merv. I had no more than 30 seconds to plead my case, so I quickly told him about Hank and the maneuver.

God bless Merv—he'd heard about it from somewhere, and seconds later, when the break was over, spontaneously, without his director, Dick Carson (yes, Johnny Carson's brother) having any warning, he introduced Hank in the audience and began asking him questions about the Heimlich maneuver. He then invited Hank up on stage to demonstrate the maneuver on him. This act of generosity brought the Heimlich maneuver to the attention of millions of people. In just a few seconds, Merv Griffin opened people's eyes and the Heimlich maneuver was on its way to opening their airways when needed. Merv's attention became the catalyst for saving thousands of lives, including former President Ronald Reagan, Cher, Elizabeth Taylor, Goldie Hawn, Walter Matthau, Carrie Fisher, and Jack Lemmon. Years later, in 1985, U.S. Surgeon General Dr. C. Everett Koop endorsed the Heimlich maneuver as the only safe method to use on a choking victim.

Thousands of people's lives have been saved since that Merv Griffin episode. Thousands continue to be saved, and will be in the future. Would I have thought to invite my uncle to sit in Merv's audience on my own? Not if I hadn't listened to the wisdom of a "simple" alcoholic janitor who loved and missed his disabled sister.

"You promise me, boy, you promise dat you gonna help people. You gonna be able to do dat. Like dey rich people here, you give back, dat's how it's 'posed to be . . . you always give back, boy, so nobody lose der family."

I kept my promise, Willie, and will always keep it.

LESSON 13

Bette Davis, a Lost Legend

"He run from hisself. Don't never run from yerself, boy."

One Sunday, I was at work dusting off some sofas in the furniture section when a murmur of excitement traveled through Leonard's. "One of the stars of *Hogan's Heroes* is looking at washers and dryers!" people whispered. In minutes, he disrupted the whole store by bringing everyone's attention to himself. Then, he turned down autograph requests. He made a scene with Howard, the appliance salesman, by insisting that he get what he wanted for free because of who he was. "Do you know who I am?" he said more than once. When Howard refused, he insisted on speaking with the owner, Fred.

To Fred's credit, he diplomatically informed the self-involved star that he would have to pay like everyone else.

"Dat's a sad man. He don't know who he is," Willie said to me, observing the situation.

"What do you mean?" I asked. I was just a kid; it would

be many years before I would truly understand what Willie meant, and just how insightful he was.

"He run from hisself. Don't never run from yerself, boy."

The star blustered for a few more minutes, and when a large enough crowd had gathered to stare, he stormed out of the store, making sure that it was a grand exit.

Fifteen years later, one of the most famous actresses in history would pull the same crap on me.

Almost from the beginning of *Happy Days*, my goal was to transition into production. I felt limited as an actor and singer, but not behind the camera. Ron Howard said that I was a natural producer, and that I should find stories that I wanted to tell. I took his advice, and for years I optioned and/or created stories. I was able to get development deals with the networks—but I never received the go-ahead to film. Truthfully, it was getting beyond discouraging.

Then late one afternoon, after visiting my parents in Burbank, I was driving past the backside of the Burbank airport. Waiting at a stoplight, I noticed a man working on an old twin-engine plane. Handing him tools was a young girl in a wheelchair. It suddenly hit me: What if a teenaged girl was constantly judged, never able to forget that she lived in a wheelchair, always made to look up? Then, what if the girl's world became everything skyward, everything free in the sky, where wheelchairs didn't exist? And what if she learned to fly, and actually looked down for the first time in her life? By the time I reached my house, the entire story about not judging and saluting the human spirit was a reality. The title: *Skyward*.

That night, I quickly wrote up *Skyward*, and then showed it to Ron the next day. He loved it and set up a meeting at

NBC to sell it. The following week, both of us were in front of Irv Wilson, the vice president of movies at NBC, pitching our hearts out. When you sell a project to the networks there are usually at least two steps: a script deal, and then a green light to go into production. Irv approved a script deal right there in the room. We were on our way, but we were still a long way from a green light.

Our first step towards green was finding the perfect screenwriter. We decided on Nancy Sackett, who was collaborative and had written some excellent, character driven scripts. Working with a writer collaboratively is important, especially for a creative producer and director team. NBC gave her their approval, she got to work, and both Ron and I gave extensive rewrite notes on every draft. While the script was coming to life, Ron and I were convinced that an actress with a physical disability, someone confined to a wheelchair, had to be cast in the lead role or our whole project would be hypocritical. We found an amazing fifteen-year-old named Suzy Gilstrap. She had never acted before, but had natural ability and charisma. She had been crippled during a fourth-grade field trip to the Los Angeles Arboretum after a large tree branch had fallen on her back. We felt so strongly about her casting that Ron acted with Suzy in a screen test to show the network after we handed in the script.

NBC loved the script, and I received my first green light to go into production.

Well, almost a green light. A cast still needed to be approved.

We set up a meeting with Brandon Tartikoff, the president of the network, to show him the screen test and plead our case for Suzy. He appreciated our passion and the cause, but reminded us that we were still in a business of ratings. He said that Melissa Sue Anderson from *Little House on the Prairie* was perfect for the part, and she guaranteed ratings. We persevered: His network could be the first in history to hire an actress with a physical disability to star in a movie! This would set an important precedent!

He thought about this and compromised. The other starring role was a retired stunt pilot—a woman who still flew and owned a café at a small airport. If we could get a commitment from an actress as famous at Bette Davis for that role, then he would approve Suzy for the other. As soon as we were out of his office, Ron and I looked at each other. Why not ask us to cast the leader of the free world? It would probably be easier. Bette Davis was still a movie star, and she had done very little television. Casting Suzy was looking very bleak.

As chance would have it, I happened to catch Bette Davis on *The Johnny Carson Show* a few nights later. She complained that all of the roles she was being offered were "old woman roles" and how she would love to do something that was against type and had some action. She also mentioned that she didn't trust her agents and insisted on reading all scripts that were submitted for her. So the next morning we crossed our fingers and messengered a script to Bette Davis's agent. What could have more action than a stunt pilot? A few days later the call came: Bette Davis loved the role and committed to the film. This was a huge coup for the network. Huge! A real event. Suzy was approved and we had a full green light.

The rest of the casting went smoothly, as did preproduction. We decided to film in Texas, and we designed the shooting schedule so that Bette Davis would finish halfway through the shoot. The week before principle photography was to begin, we received word that Davis wanted cartons of Marlboro Reds and a case of expensive scotch in her room upon arrival.

That should have been our first warning sign.

Early evening, a few days before the first day of shooting, Davis arrived. We had her picked up in a limo and planned to meet in her hotel suite that night. Ron could only stay a short time because of prior commitments related to the project. When she met us at the door, Marlboro in hand, her first words were, "Babies! You're both babies!" She then rambled on about how much we didn't know, that now she was nervous about making this film . . . yada, yada, yada. It was clear to me that she had already dipped into the scotch. Ron excused himself and now it was me, alone with the legend, for the duration. She insisted that I have a drink with her, which turned into several. I learned that she could hold her liquor, and I realized that she was trying to get me blasted.

Filming got under way, and Ron did a great job directing her, but he was limited because of her acting style. Not a word of dialogue could be changed for her or anybody else in the scene. Everything had to be exactly as rehearsed; there was absolutely no room for a spontaneous moment. Her drinking also made her unpredictable and Ron and I were always on edge, waiting for Bette Davis's Next Meltdown. At the end of one shooting day, she dropped her guard a bit and confided in me that she was selfish, a terrible mother, and that she would die alone at the top of a hill. From my standpoint, I wasn't about to disagree.

Davis had a day off before her last day on the set. For almost two weeks of shooting, this was the first day that she wasn't working and it was wonderful. Everybody was having a grand time in her absence, despite the fact that Texas was suffering through a record-setting heat wave. We were shooting at a small airport in the city of Rockwall, and late in the afternoon I was told there was a call for me. I took it in the small, one-man office we had. "Hello?" I said.

"I'm not dying for you sons of bitches!" screamed a voice across the line.

"What?" I responded. It was Bette Davis.

"I'm not dying for you sons of bitches! Have you seen the paper?!"

I quickly found that day's paper on the office desk. The headline read something like "Seven Elderly Dead From Heat Wave."

Davis continued, "Tomorrow, I want the entire airport tarped! I will be bringing a thermometer. The minute it hits 100 degrees, I am walking!"

Then she hung up.

Stunned, I ran back across the airport where Ron was shooting to tell him the news. We didn't have the time or money to tarp an airport, so we quickly decide to hire an extra camera and crew the next day so we could finish her work as early as possible. Ron redesigned and simplified his shots in order to pull it off. The entire climax of the movie would be compromised, but there was nothing that we could do.

The next day the temperature soared. At 8 in the morning, true to her word, Davis walked on set, theatrically placed a thermometer on the camera dolly, and then said, "Time to rehearse."

We put a tarp above her head but it was obvious that before we had our first shot in the can it was already over 100 degrees. Unexpectedly, Davis said nothing and Ron was able to get her done in a few hours. We brought her flowers, thanked her, and—truth be told—couldn't get her off the set fast enough. But she had one more manipulative, self-serving game to play. She turned to the cast and crew and said, "Oh no, I can't go! I must stay here to speak my off-camera lines for my fellow actors."

No one present for these scenes knew of the problems we'd been having with her, so everyone thought that she was amazing, working in the heat to help her fellow thespians, a real pro. They didn't realize that she had bastardized the climax of the film and made Ron's and my life pure hell. Sure enough, she stayed until the very last shot, blowing kisses to the crew as she departed, heading off to torture new victims. Watching her ride away, I felt an overwhelming sadness.

"Dat's a sad man. He don't know who he is. He run from hisself."

She will die on a mountaintop, alone, I thought. She will never know who she was. She never had the courage to find out. She is a made-up illusion, forever running away, never stopping to face her true self.

LESSON 14

Please Come With Me, Sir

"He make me feel dat I important."

It was Friday after school, and I was late for work. Racing into the janitorial room, there was Willie, grease-stained cigarette between his lips, talking with the mayor of Burbank, George Haven. Both were sitting on the dust-ridden oil drum cans. It turned out that years before, Willie had saved George from a couple of thugs in the store's parking lot, and they'd been friends ever since.

"George, dis 'ere's Anson," Willie introduced me.

"Anson dis 'ere's George, who be yer mayor."

We said our hellos and George had to run, but not before he said to me, "You listen to our man, Willie, here. He's very special to all of us."

The mayor left and Willie got out his dented flask. "The mayor's a nice guy," I said.

"He know how to lead," Willie said, putting his flask down. "He make me feel dat I important."

I didn't know yet, but Willie had just described the truest purpose of a real leader.

★ ★ ★

I received a call from the National Association of Student Leaders (NASL) soon after *Skyward* premiered. Despite the difficulties with Bette Davis, it was a critical and ratings success. It also broke open opportunities for actors with disabilities, and the NASL felt that *Skyward* represented unsung, selfless leaders who inspired others and gave them the strength to overcome adversity. Every year the association holds a national convention that includes the top student leaders from across America—student body presidents, heads of student councils, the cream of the crop. They invited me to give the keynote speech that year at Shawnee Mission High School, in Shawnee Mission, Kansas. Having never been elected to anything, I was humbled and honored.

Writing the speech, I thought back to the things Willie taught me about leadership in the "Dey Talk Room," and I realized it was important to me to share Willie's wisdom, to instill it in the hearts of these young leaders. I felt that they could be more, inspire more, and give more, if they, like me, were motivated by the lessons of Willie Turner.

A few days before the event, I received a phone call from one of the committee members asking me for my Social Security number and other personal information. It turned out that the President of the United States, Ronald Reagan, was using the event to give his speech on education, and the White House needed to clear all of the major participants. I said that I was not comfortable being part of a political event, but they assured me that I would be delivering my keynote to the students in the auditorium an hour before the President would appear in the school's large gymnasium to deliver his speech, so in fact it was a completely different event.

I flew to Kansas the night before my speech, so I was able to spend quality time with many of the student leaders. To say that I was impressed was an understatement. The young men and women were smart, worldly, and gifted, and, most importantly, they all wanted to better people's lives.

The keynote went well. During the question-and-answer session, numerous questions were asked about Willie, and it was clear to me that his insights hit a major chord with the entire room.

Afterwards, the committee chairman asked if I'd like to hear the President's speech. "Sure," I said. We walked over to the massive gymnasium, and went through a quick security check. We were then seated close to the stage.

The gym was packed with an eclectic group and the national press was there. You could feel the anticipation in that gym, and when President Reagan stepped onto the stage the place exploded in cheers and applause. His charisma electrified the room. He began speaking, and during an applause interruption, he glanced over at me and smiled. Startled, I think that I gave him a geeky wave.

At the end of his speech, which was terrific, the room went wild. As the crowd was clearing out, I was asked if I'd like to be in the receiving line to shake hands with the President. Excited, I said yes. I was escorted to a line of about forty people. After waiting a few minutes, a Secret Service agent walked up to me. "Please come with me, sir."

I immediately thought that I was marked as a security risk or something. Walking with him down a typical high school hallway, with lockers and classrooms on each side of us, I nervously asked, "Where we going?"

He replied, "The President would like to meet you."

I instantly lost my breath. I was going to meet the leader of the free world! We stopped outside a nondescript classroom. The agent opened the door, and there was President Reagan, speaking on a briefcase phone. He noticed me, smiled, and then held up his hand to indicate we should hold on for a minute. The agent closed the door. The next few moments seemed like forever. It was all I could do not to hyperventilate, and I could hardly speak when I was finally escorted into the normal, class-sized room. Through a wall of windows opposite me, I could see the Presidential motorcade parked on the street, flags rippling in the wind. Then President Reagan walked up to me. "I can't thank you enough, Anson, for meeting with me," he said, as he shook my hand and warmly held my arm with his other.

In ten seconds, the President had made me feel "dat I important." He told me how much he liked *Happy Days*, the songs I sang, and the memories it brought back to him.

Oh my God! I thought. The President actually watches the show.

He then told me the reason he wanted to meet. He was frustrated because his schedule and security wouldn't allow him to spend time with the young leaders who were attending the conference. He said that these kids are our future and it was important for him to hear their voices and maybe learn a thing or two. He had recognized me during his speech, and when he found out that I gave the keynote address and had spent time with the students he asked to speak with me. He wanted me to brief him on the event, the student leaders, and their visions for the future of America.

For twenty minutes, I told him about the amazing young men and women, their courageous stories, their impressive accomplishments, and their selfless desire to genuinely help people. One particular story actually brought tears to his eyes. A seventeen-year-old Hispanic girl, Lucia, from New Mexico, was student body president and a top honor student. She also worked thirty hours a week, after school and weekends, as a motel maid to help support her single mom and a younger brother. Her mom had beaten heroin, but had sustained life-threatening damage to her health as a result. She worked at the same motel. Together, they made enough money to rent a small house and put food on the table. In her limited spare time, Lucia made sure to tutor her twelve-year-old brother, who was also a straight 'A' student. The President took a pen and small paper out from his coat and wrote down "Lucia/New Mexico."

"We have programs for special individuals like her and her family. She's been a maid long enough."

At this point, one of the agents was signaling the President that they had to go. This time, instead of shaking my hand, President Reagan gave me a hug, and thanked me again for taking the time to meet.

Walking back down that high school hallway, I thought about Willie and the President of the United States. I thought about Lucia, and how wonderful it was that her life and her family's life was going to change, and how lucky we were to have a President in office who was selfless, and who honestly cared about us and our country's future.

"He know how to lead. He make me feel dat I important."

LESSON 15

One Funky-Looking, Small Plaque

"Dose words can save everythin'."

Willie was illiterate, but he kept an old Irish saying, written on a yellowed, worn piece of paper, taped on his "Talk Room" wall. He explained it to me: Years earlier he was delivering a refrigerator, and part of his job was to take away the old one to dispose of it. When he got the old fridge in the truck, he spotted a note that had fallen down and gotten stuck in the door. Something moved him to keep it, and back at the store a cashier on lunch break read it to him: "There is no limit to what a man can do or where he can go if he does not mind who gets the credit." Then he said to me, "Boy, dose words can save everythin'. No mo' wars, no one hungry, all people's happy."

★ ★ ★

Quite a few years after I met with President Reagan, he was still in office. *Happy Days* was going strong, and I'd been fortunate in producing and writing more television. One day, while waiting at a car wash, I was looking through the books in the store area of the service station. I happened upon a paperback titled *First Lady's Lady*, by Sheila Weidenfeld. Sheila was Betty Ford's press secretary, and her book was about living in two worlds: working with the most powerful couple in the world, then rushing home to supervise her kids' homework and dinner. It was fun and relatable, and reminded me of a Mary Tyler Moore-type show. I showed it to Ron, and we both agreed that it could be a great movie of the week, and then a weekly comedy series.

We contacted Sheila and optioned the book. We then met with NBC and they made a script deal with us. A gifted writer, Michael Bortman, was hired to do the screenplay, and he asked us if it was possible to visit the East Wing of the White House to get a better feel for Sheila's world. We spoke with Sheila, and not only did she get us approval to tour the East Wing, she also set up a meeting for us with a second Sheila—Sheila Tate, who was Nancy Reagan's press secretary at that time.

Growing up, the only politician I'd met was the mayor of Burbank. I was fifteen and I thought he was the only one I'd ever meet. In fact, he was the only one that I needed to meet, because that encounter resulted in Willie teaching me the definition of real leadership. It's been startling over the years to realize how many powerful politicians are definitely not leaders—I've met presidents, senators, and congressmen who are only out for themselves, golden calves who will tell any story to stay in power. Truthfully, the only politician I have ever met (on a national level) who was a real leader was President Reagan.

On a beautiful Washington day, Sheila Weidenfeld, Ron, Michael, and I rode through the gates of the White House. Once inside, we were escorted to the East Wing for our meeting with Sheila Tate. The First Lady's domain was calm and serene. Both Sheilas were wonderful, and they gave our writer, Michael Bortman, lots of information. Then they took him on a detailed tour of the East Wing.

Once back in Sheila Tate's office, she asked Ron and me if we'd like to meet President Reagan. I didn't mention my past experience. We were whisked through the building and into the waiting corridor outside the Oval Office. We then went through a door to a small waiting room, where we met the President's personal secretary, Kathleen Osborne. She apologized profusely, saying that the President wasn't in, that he had to leave for meetings. Ron and I were already thrilled to be in such close proximity to the most famous office in the world. Kathleen then said, "I shouldn't do this, but," and she opened the entry door and said, "Go on in. You can have a couple of minutes."

The next thing we knew, she closed the door behind us, and Ron and I were alone in the Oval office. This was before cell phones with cameras, and I wanted to remember everything about this extraordinary moment. We took in the stunning Remington sculptures and the priceless paintings. We slowly walked around the room toward the President's desk. Later on, I learned Queen Victoria gave it to our country. On this day, the President's desk was pristine and polished to a high gloss, everything was perfectly in place except for one funky-looking small plaque standing close to his phone. Curious, I started to walk around to the front of the desk to read it, but before I could I heard, "We have to go now."

Kathryn was ushering us out.

Many years later, in 2004, President Reagan passed away and numerous television tributes aired in honor of his passing. On the day of his funeral, I happened to tune in to a rerun of Nancy Reagan hosting a tour of the Ronald Reagan Library on PBS. She was in the library's "Oval Office," explaining that it was an exact replica of President Reagan's. She went on to say that the furnishings were duplicates, but that all of his personal items were authentic. As she was crossing to his desk I saw it: the funky plaque that I didn't get the chance to read! She picked it up and said that it was Ronnie's most important personal keepsake. He'd had it on his desk when he was the Screen Actors Guild president, the governor of California, and the president of the United States of America. It was an old Irish saying, and he would never start an important call or meeting without reading it first. Ever. "There is no limit to what a man can do or where he can go if he does not mind who gets the credit."

It was a moment that was difficult to wrap my mind around. The words Willie lived by were the same words that the leader of the free world lived by. Two great teachers and two great men, one in a janitorial room and one on the world stage—and both have created legacies that live on. "Dose words can save everythin'. No mo' wars, no one hungry, all people's happy."

You are so right, Willie.

LESSON 16

My "Big Room" Break from the Best

"Dat song make me feel alive, but only when Sammy sing it. He got mo' pain den me, but he take mine away."

Growing up, Dino, Desi, and Billy was a popular teen group. Dino was Dean Martin's son, Desi was Lucille Ball and Desi Arnaz's son, and Billy was a close friend of theirs. At the time, they were on the cover of every teen magazine in the world. I would sit on my small front porch, reading a magazine, dreaming about driving one of their Ferraris and having girls run after me. I never realized that one day I'd be in the same publication, and actually meet and spend time with both Dino and Desi.

It wasn't until years later that I learned their lives were not as great as the magazines projected. It turns out, we were pretty much alike—me, a kid sitting in front of a one-bathroom house, just a number in the world, and them, sons of superstars, rich and famous. Like me, they didn't have the love in their lives that they so desperately needed. It doesn't matter how rich and famous you are, there is no happiness without the love of family.

Actually, I was the lucky one, because I had to work hard jobs to earn money. My parents never had more than a hundred dollars in savings, and I had to pay for everything that I ever wanted except for food and basic clothes. If I didn't have to work, I never would have met Willie. It's ironic that with all the cars, fame and money, Dino and Desi kept searching for happiness, but a simple, uneducated janitor found me mine.

It was in one of those teen magazines that I first learned about the Rat Pack and Sammy Davis, Jr. Dino Martin was talking about his dad, Dean, and the Vegas shows he did with Frank Sinatra, Sammy Davis, and Joey Bishop. Dean Martin said that Sammy was the most talented in their group, the best nightclub performer in the world. I didn't have much interest in nightclubs, Sammy, or the others in the pack at the time, but years later, I would get my "Big Room" break from "The Best."

Elvis was Willie's number one favorite performer, this is true. But honestly the Rat Pack could be considered an equal number one. He loved Frank Sinatra, Dean Martin, Joey Bishop, and, especially, Sammy Davis, Jr. Their music would instantly soften his face and put a smile in his eyes, and when he'd bring in his ancient record player and play their 33 LPs and 45s, the song that he played over and over again was "Birth of the Blues" sung by Sammy. "Dat song make me feel alive, but only when Sammy sing it. He got mo' pain den me, but he take mine away."

When I was his janitorial assistant, I was too young to

understand the perceptiveness of his words. Willie understood that Sammy helped everybody but himself; that he used
his pain—and ultimately, that is what made him great. Willie
was teaching me that those who tap into immense talent must
also reach into the depths of their own emotions, both good
and bad. If you didn't find that balance, the bad could destroy
you. The evidence abounds: Marilyn Monroe, Billie Holiday,
Janis Joplin, Jim Morrison, Vincent Van Gogh. I listened to
what he was saying, but honestly, at fifteen I didn't get it. I
wished my parents were rich and I wanted the fast car and
the girls.

★ ★ ★

Singing on *Happy Days* opened a whole new world for me.
For years, we would shoot a show on a Friday night and afterward I would immediately drive to the airport to catch a
red-eye to the city I was performing a concert in the next
day. I'd fly back on a Sunday and be back on set on Monday.
The gigs were mostly at large state fairs and amusement parks,
like Disneyland and Six Flags. I had a lot of fun and met so
many amazing people, but I wanted to continue performing
and it occurred to me that I had better progress to adult venues, like Vegas, Reno, and Atlantic City. The thing was, the
"Big Rooms" considered me a teenybopper performer and
not right for their clientele. I tried, but I couldn't even get
near the door, let alone get a foot inside. My agent wouldn't
give up, though, and then one day the call I was hoping for
came. Sammy Davis, Jr. was performing with Bill Cosby at
Harrah's in Reno, and he needed four nights off during his
engagement. He had approved me as his replacement. In min-

utes my career turned around—I was headlining with Bill Cosby in the "Big Room"!

I had exactly had three weeks to put an entirely new show together. Thank God I was opening and only needed 30 minutes of material.

In no time, it was time to depart for Reno. I went with my conductor, Richard Barron, and our rhythm section. We were all treated like royalty upon arrival. The suite they gave me was right out of a movie: two floors high, four bedrooms, five bathrooms, a movie screen that came down from the ceiling electronically, and a full bar. The most incredible touch was a full buffet, served in polished sterling silver by a white-gloved server (I later found out that all meals were serviced and served this way).

I had a terrific rehearsal with the orchestra and then I was taken back to Sammy's (my temporary) dressing room. I can still picture it: There was a decked-out meeting area, a full bar, a bedroom, and a huge bathroom. To top it off, during my performances I would have the services of Sammy's valet and bartender too. I felt like part of the pack, like I should be scanning the place for Frank, Dean, and Joey.

On my opening night, I was buzzing with adrenaline. Bill Cosby came into my dressing room to wish me luck. What a great man, I thought, going out of his way like this to make me feel like an equal. He calmed my nerves by doing so.

Still, it was slightly overwhelming. I planned to start the show from the back of the house, and then move through the audience to the stage. So after the room was seated, I took my wireless mike and waited just outside the front entrance for my cue. I heard my booming introduction, and was through the door singing "Tossin' and Turnin'", shaking hands and dancing with the ladies on my way to the stage.

At the start of the second verse, I was looking into the crowd when the spotlight hit one man: Sammy Davis, Jr.! For an instant the words, everything went away and I felt supreme shock. Sammy is in the audience? Sammy is in the audience! Somehow I managed to get to the stage and back on track, but rest of the show was a blur. I think I received a nice ovation at the end. Back in the dressing room, I still couldn't figure out why I was there to take Sammy's place if he was at Harrah's too.

"Where's my man? Where's my man?" I heard. The door opened and there was Sammy in person. He walked in and gave me a bear hug before telling me what a great job I did. I wasn't certain if he really meant it, but he sure made me feel special. We each got a glass of wine and sat down to talk. I asked him why he was there, since I was told he needed time off. He explained that he was going through some scheduled medical tests and it was recommended that he not perform until they were complete. It didn't mean that he couldn't watch my opening night. He said that he had seen me on *The Merv Griffin Show*, and thought that I had potential. So when he learned he would need a temporary fill-in and my name came up, he called Merv (a close friend of his) who said nice things about me.

I'd had no idea that all of this went on before I was booked.

We talked for quite a while. I told him about Willie, and how much Willie loved him. Sammy was touched, but unlike Elvis, Sammy never had a friend who could help him with his problems. He told me that his life as a kid was hard, that he didn't have a family life, and that he had to perform to make people smile. No one was there to offer him help. What he said next put me right back with Willie in "Dey Talk Room." Sammy confided that the only time his emptiness went away was when he saw smiles in the audience and heard the applause at the end of a song. For him, that was a moment in time when all was perfect.

Before he left, Sammy gave me one more bear hug. Like family.

After the gig at Harrah's Reno, I received an offer from Resorts International in Atlantic City to co-headline with the beautiful and talented Lola Falana. I knew that Sammy had discovered Lola and that they were great friends. I didn't think that booking was any coincidence. Sammy had quietly made my second "Big Room" opportunity happen. "Dat song make me feel alive, but only when Sammy sing it. He got mo' pain den me, but he take mine away." You were so right, Willie, but it also took away Sammy's. That's why he lived to perform: His family was his audience.

No Greater Gift

"You go with yer feelins, boy.
Don't get stuck like deez people."

In Atlantic City I was treated like royalty, and Lola Falana was beyond gracious. The shows were going great, the reviews were positive, and the attendance was 100 percent. Still, in my gut, I felt something was off. My agent was in negotiations with The Sahara Hotel and Casino in Vegas for my next show, but on the final night in Atlantic City, as I was waiting for my intro, my mind heard Willie instead: "You go with yer feelins, boy. Don't get stuck like deez people."

He had said that to me once, referring to many coworkers at Leonard's. They didn't look or act happy. It was obvious that the store was not where they were destined to be, but they now had no choice.

"Go with yer feelins . . ." As I was walking onto the stage, I knew in my heart that it would be my last time. My "feelins" said that I should move on, that this part of my destiny was complete. The next day, I called my agent and he grudgingly canceled negotiations with The Sahara. I never looked back. I set my sights on getting off the stage and spending my time behind the camera, writing and producing. It just felt right. Soon I had numerous projects in development.

One day while speaking with Ron, I confided that while producing was great, it made me feel detached, like I was no longer a true part of the creative process. Ron recommended that I do something that scared me: direct. Producing and directing are two different worlds. As a producer, you are all business. But as director, you're constantly making decisions that impact the creative side of the project: casting, choosing locations, wardrobe, crew, set design, and on and on. I worried if I could handle it. Ron reminded me that I had spent years observing the best directors on the Paramount lot: John Schlesinger, Roman Polanski, and John Badham (and of course, Ron. I had watched Ron too). He convinced me that I could handle it and that I would do well.

Coincidentally, an *Afterschool Special* I had co-created called *No Greater Gift* was "green lit" soon after our conversation. It was about two twelve-year-old boys, one Hispanic and one African American, who meet in a hospital and become quick friends. After one child learns that he is terminally ill, he makes a pact to save his friend's life through organ donation. Acting on Ron's advice, I made an appointment with my ABC executive to convince her to let me hire myself. It wasn't an easy task. Even though I was the project's executive producer and co-creator, the approval to direct as well was not immediate. After some negotiation, and after Ron agreed to oversee (and take over if I was having trouble), I was finally approved. Ron's friendship and belief in me was a great gift.

Betty Thomas, who was on *Hill Street Blues* at the time, agreed to a starring role in the film (today she is one of the most respected feature directors in the world). We found two sensational young actors, Ajay Naidu and Zero Hubbard, to play the kids, and a terrific supporting cast. From the first shooting day we were blessed, almost like an outside hand was guiding us. Sure, trying to analyze every question coming at me was exhausting, but whenever I thought I was reaching my breaking point, "Go with yer feelins" came into my head. There was Willie, and everything calmed down after that. I found a rhythm and confidence.

After a few days, the network made a surprise visit to the *No Greater Gift* set, congratulating everybody on great dailies, and telling us how important the film was to ABC. I learned that I was now on the director-approved list.

Ajay and Zero had lots of life questions. We were working together on very sensitive material, and even though they were in very responsible positions, they were still kids who needed guidance. I enjoyed our talks as much as I enjoyed filming and tried to help them, like Willie helped me.

The purpose of the film was to humanize organ donation. At the time people were wary of it because of the imagery surrounding the process. The cast, crew, and I were hoping that our little film might open people's hearts and change this. Before the show's credits ran, we provided contact information to help viewers get more facts on donation. *No Greater Gift* aired in September of 1985 to great reviews, and the results were stunning: Organ donation went up as a direct result of the film! For years, *No Greater Gift* helped give the gift of life to thousands of individuals in need.

"You go with yer feelins, boy."

I did, and in just a year, I won the Humanitas Award as a writer, became a director, and, most importantly, was part of a film that saved the lives of many wonderful people in need . . . all because of your guidance, Willie.

LESSON 18

The Lone Star Kid

*"You gonna do somethin' great in life.
Just a feelin' I got."*

I turned on CNN one morning and watched a story about the youngest mayor in the history of the United States. His name was Brian Zimmerman; he was eleven years old, and mayor of his hometown of Crabb, Texas. Getting elected was an amazing achievement, but what caught my interest were this young man's accomplishments. Once he was mayor, he not only convinced Houston (Crabb is in its jurisdiction) to put in paved roads, he also created an ambulance and security service for Crabb. I wanted to option the rights to Brian's story, so I flew to Crabb to meet with Brian and his parents.

They were an impressive family. His dad dropped out of law school to go into the ranching and restaurant business. His mom worked with his dad, and both made sure that they were there for their son. Brian was beyond his years in maturity, yet still a kid. He had a pet turkey named Drumstick and used a go-cart to get around town.

I wanted to know what had motivated Brian to achieve so much while he was still so young. It turned out that he had witnessed a horrible car accident. A driver was injured badly—he was bleeding out, and the nearest emergency and ambulance service was almost an hour away. Help arrived, but only after the young man had died. Witnessing this had a profound effect on Brian. He realized that the man's life could have been saved if there had been an emergency service located in Crabb.

On his own he started reading his dad's old law books. He discovered that the way to create an emergency service in their community was to form an unincorporated town. To do this, an election needed to be held in Crabb, and a mayor elected. Brian's best friend was a kid named Moses; but he had relied most upon an older African American man by the name of Holmes. Brian told me that Holmes was "blind and illiterate, and the smartest man I know." Whenever he had problems or had trouble figuring out his life, Holmes had just the right words to help Brian move forward. I was taken aback; it was as if Willie had a twin brother.

Brian had talked to Holmes about making Crabb a better place, and Holmes had told him that he should lead. Brian thought that was crazy advice, but Holmes said, "I got a feelin'," practically the same words that Willie had once told me. He convinced Brian to put together an election and run. Holmes made his living by selling junk; he used all of his savings, $150, to finance Brian's campaign. Numerous candidates ran for mayor, and it was no secret that many felt an eleven-year-old boy running was an embarrassing joke. When Brian got discouraged, Holmes reminded him to go with his feelins, and that the purpose of life was to "go down proud." Brian won the election, but it was a bittersweet victory for him because days later Holmes passed away from a heart attack.

As mayor, Brian made Crabb a better place. He arranged for Houston to repair roads, he created a volunteer emergency medical and security service; it was amazing to see what a selfless leader could accomplish. For me, Brian's story was a microcosm for Washington—the progress our country could make if we followed the goals of our founding fathers without personal agendas.

Brian and his family let me option the rights to Brian's story. Ron and I were executive producers, and we sold *The Lone Star Kid* to a PBS show called *Wonderworks*. They aired amazing films that lifted the human spirit and made them on a shoestring budget. I cowrote the screenplay, and soon after we were given a green light to film. Our casting budget was small, so we planned to hire mostly unknown actors. We found Chad Sheets, who was brilliant as Brian Zimmerman, and we were fortunate to get Charlie Daniels to play the antagonist, the man who ran against Brian. (In actuality, seven people ran against him, but we thought it best dramatically to just have one.) Charlie was fantastic in the role, and he also wrote two songs and the entire film score for free. On a wing and a prayer, we sent James Earl Jones the script to consider the part of Holmes. Even though the budget only allowed minimum scale, James said yes, and brought our project up to a whole new level.

I couldn't help but write Holmes very much like Willie. Even though I had never met him, to my mind they had the same voice and heart. Then the first day James worked, it was as if he reincarnated Willie. He had a bit of a southern tone to his delivery . . . but he was Willie. We filmed in McDade, Texas, but were able to bring in Brian and a lot of Crabb's residents for cameos. It was a quick eight-day shoot, and we made a wonderful movie. It got great promotion and aired to excellent reviews. It also won numerous awards, and brought well-deserved attention to Brian and his achievements.

Afterward, I wondered if anyone understood the underlying message of the film. I found out when Poland was transitioning into a democracy. PBS informed me that the Polish constitutional committee had requested a copy of The Lone Star Kid to screen. They felt the film represented the purest example of democracy. I was speechless. My grandmother had escaped Poland before World War I, and now I was a small part of its rebirth. I thought back to the first day I met Willie and he said to me, "You gonna do somethin' great in life. Just a feelin' I got."

Well, I discovered that it takes a joining together of noble hearts to do something great. Without Holmes, Brian would never have run for mayor; and without Willie, I would have never done the film.

On a sad note, Brian Zimmerman passed away from a heart attack on September 6, 1996. He was 24 years old. Chad Sheets, the actor who portrayed him, passed away after a battle with cancer on December 24, 1998. He was 26 years old. Both were leaders born in August, and both did "go down proud," making the world a better place.

The Worst Script Ever

"You need surprises. Dey wake you up."

One evening, Fred, the owner of Leonard's, surprised all of his workers with a free movie night. The film was *Harper*, starring Paul Newman. It was playing across town at the California Theater in Burbank. Fred was generous: He provided a bus for transportation and let all of us buy whatever snacks we wanted. Willie, stuffing down popcorn smothered with butter, was the most excited. He loved Paul Newman, and would go on and on about him. "Some people's just posed to be seen by everbody. Dey gots dat thing."

The first day I worked with Henry Winkler, it was so clear that he had that something that connected him to everybody. Most recently, I recognized it when I directed the talented Shailene Woodley in *The Secret Life of the American Teenager*. She truly "gots dat thing."

A movie that was a smash hit while we were making *Happy Days* was *Star Wars*. Garry Marshall's ten-year-old son,

Scotty, saw it and asked his dad to do a *Happy Days* episode with an alien in it. A Martian episode. Garry thought that it was a fun idea and assigned one of his staff to write the script. We had a pretty set schedule during a normal workweek. Mondays we'd have a cast reading of that week's script, and then a reading of the following week's script so that the writers could get a jump on it. The Monday that we had the first reading of the Martian script "Mork From Ork" is memorable to me, because to say it stunk is too kind. It was the worst script of the entire run of the show, and nothing was even a close second. We all complained, but Garry assured us that it would be fine after they had a chance to rewrite.

The following Monday was the shooting week of the "Mork" episode. Again we read it, and again it was horrid. No one wanted to be part of it, but what could we do? The show had to be shot. A character actor was cast as Mork. He was terrible. Actually, it wasn't his fault; the part was not actable. This actor was so embarrassed by that Wednesday's rehearsal that he walked off the set, never to return. He had quit and this presented a huge problem: Thursday was camera-blocking day, and Friday we had to shoot the show in front of a live audience. Garry called an emergency meeting on the set and asked if any of us knew of a funny actor who was available. Al Molinaro, who played Al on the show, said that there was a guy in his Harvey Lembeck improvisational class who might work; it turned out Garry's sister, Ronnie, who was in casting, knew him, too, and agreed. Garry cast him sight unseen, and we all went home counting the hours for this episode to be over, done, finished. The actor's name was Robin Williams.

When I got to the stage the next day, I felt a sense of excitement—like a powerful energy—even before I opened the door. This was puzzling, because I was headed in to block the Worst Script Ever. Then I opened the door and was amazed to see every writer for *Happy Days* huddled around the set. You have to understand: It was camera-blocking day. This is the time we worked on the mechanics of setting the camera shots for a live audience show. There was never a writer present, and yet on this day every one of them was there. And looking thrilled.

What's going on? I wondered.

Jerry Paris, our director, ran up to me saying, "He's a genius! He's a genius!"

I joined the crowd of writers and there was Robin Williams, rehearsing and improvising the entire show by the millisecond. I watched him instantaneously create "Nanu, Nanu!" the Orkan greeting, sit on his head, and on and on. The writers were furiously writing down all that he invented. Robin was electrifying, a true genius, and all I could think was, "Man, he's got a lot of 'dat thing'!"

It turned out that what was the worst *Happy Days* episode on Wednesday turned into the best by Friday night, all because of the brilliance of Robin Williams. At the end of the show the audience went wild. They must have given Robin an uninterrupted ten-minute standing ovation. I had never, ever witnessed such a spontaneous explosion of connection between a performer and an audience. Truly, a superstar was born.

Time, place, and genius took Robin onto the world's stage. He fits his own creative mold, not anyone else's. If he hadn't found a vehicle where he could invent, would he have ever been truly discovered?

Robin is one of the nicest people that I've ever worked with, a sensitive and caring man.* As soon as the "Mork" show was ready, Garry Marshall took clips of Robin's performance and put them together with clips of Pam Dawber, from an unsold pilot that he had produced, and created a presentation for a series entitled *Mork and Mindy.* Fred Silverman, president of ABC, bought thirteen episodes and the rest is history. Willie used to say, "You need surprises. Dey wake you up." Robin Williams sure woke me up and taught me that there is always something that can be made out of whatever hand you are dealt. "Some people's just 'posed to be seen by everbody. Dey gots dat thing."

---

*As this book was going to press, the world lost the great genius Robin Williams. Robin was put on this earth to wake us up. His comedy made us laugh, but more importantly, made us think. His enormous talent, widespread generosity and deep compassion went far beyond a physical body. His spirit will live on and continue to inspire people. I am so thankful to have known him.

LESSON 20

I'd Be Bothered with Me Too

"Dere's people dat help you and den go away . . .
dey important."

The year was 1964 and I was in junior high school. President Kennedy had been assassinated five months prior, and people were still feeling the tragic loss of Camelot. My friend Jeff Schredder and I were on Easter break, and we wanted to go to the Teenage Fair. It was a yearly event held at the Hollywood Palladium in Los Angeles. It was fun and uplifting and catered to teenagers with current trend booths, rides, and music acts. Jeff and I were driven there by his mom and dropped off.

We escaped from the sad mood of the country into the feel-good vibe of the event. The duo Sonny & Cher and the group Frankie Valli and the Four Seasons were both scheduled to perform. Jeff and I watched as Sonny & Cher sang a few of their current hits. I thought they were gimmicky, but entertaining. After their short concert, we ate our way through the fair, going on rides and having a great time.

After a few hours, we headed back to the stage just in time for Frankie Valli and the Four Seasons. We were lucky enough to stand right down front. Frankie came out and lit up the early evening. He was amazing. Toward the end of his show, he took a moment and talked about President Kennedy. I was close enough to see tears in his eyes and I felt them spring to mine. He then closed the show with a heartfelt ballad. When he stepped off of the stage, he passed right by me. Then he stopped and turned back, placing his hand on my shoulder. I was hurting, and without saying one word, he took some of my grief at the loss of the president away. He then disappeared backstage. Willie would say, "Dere's people dat help you and den go away . . . dey important." It took me years to understand what he meant.

★ ★ ★

After I got a record deal with Chelsea Records (the same label that David Cassidy was signed to) Garry was instrumental in letting "the band" (it never got a name) premiere whatever single we decided to release on *Happy Days*. There were big challenges along the way. One was finding the right songs; the other was learning how to record them.

Luckily, for the first challenge we had a huge advantage: Charles Fox and Norman Gimbel, the team that wrote the *Happy Days* theme song (as well as some of the greatest songs ever written: "Killing Me Softly," "I Got A Name," and "Ready To Take A Chance Again" are a few) came on board to write for me. What an experience it was to work with these two legends! They were geniuses; no other word can describe their talent.

As for the second challenge, Charlie Calello was hired as my producer. Charlie not only produced Frankie Valli, the man who touched my heart (and my shoulder!) when I was a teen, but also Barbra Streisand, Neil Diamond, Bruce Springsteen—his list was incredible. We had a few rehearsals to help me find my recording voice (I'm still looking) and then I went into the studio. I have to admit that I was quite intimidated by Charlie. He was the best who worked with the best, and I truly felt that I had no reason to be behind that microphone.

The first night we didn't get a thing recorded, I was just too insecure. I became fifteen again, ready to fail and lose. The next night wasn't any better, and I could tell that Charlie was bothered. I didn't blame him. I'd be bothered with me too. Finally Charlie called for a meal break. He said they'd bring food into the studio so that the rest of us (all the technical people who were watching me blow it) didn't have to leave, and then he took off on an errand. I had no appetite, and wandered over to an adjoining studio to be by myself. My recording career was dead and buried before it was even born. After sulking for about 30 minutes, I felt a hand on my shoulder. There was something oddly familiar, something echoing back in time. I turned around and there was Frankie Valli! "Charlie asked me to come down and see if I could maybe help you a bit," he said.

I was dumbfounded. It turned out that Charlie was not only Frankie's producer, but also his best friend. Charlie hadn't been bothered by my lack of ability; he was bothered by the unnecessary stress that I was putting myself through. So he had called Frankie to see if he could help me out, and that he did. Frankie gestured to all of the people in the other room. "Forget they're there," he suggested. "Picture that one girl you care about and sing just to her. Get everything else out of your mind." He went on to give me a master's degree in recording in less than 20 minutes.

An assistant walked in, letting me know that it was time to get back to work. Frankie said that he would hang out for a bit.

This time in the studio everything went great. I recorded a few takes and then Charlie had me come into the booth. I could tell that everybody was thrilled at my improvement. Frankie was gone. Charlie said that he had to do something with one of his kids. I never saw Frankie again, and I never got the chance to tell him that we had met once before. Maybe he remembered? All I know for certain is that I finally understood what Willie was trying to tell me when he said, "Dere's people dat help you and den go away . . . dey important." He wanted me to be open for charmed teachers. For people like Frankie Valli. For those chosen few who come into your life briefly, when you need help, so that you can move forward.

Hi, I'm Brad Pitt

"All dat matters is dey good dat goes on after you gone."

You can tell a lot about a person's character by how much they give of themselves. Do they take the time for others, have an open heart, and give before they take? Selfish salesmen and customers at the store bothered Willie; he would call them "de users." He felt deeply that living a self-serving, limited life hurt everyone and everything around you. He was a pay-it-forward kind of man—to him, this was the meaning and purpose of our existence. Willie lived his life walking this walk; you reading this book, in fact, is Willie paying it forward. He told me many times, "All dat matters is dey good dat goes on after you gone. Don't never forget dat, boy." He taught me to be aware of exceptional people, the ones who do move humanity to a better place.

After I got on the approved list I was able to build a successful career directing television. Steven Bochco gave me a big break, hiring me to direct *LA Law,* and Jay Tarses hired me to direct *The Slap Maxwell Story*. In turn, these two shows opened up several more directing opportunities, including movies of the week for NBC. Then my agent called one day with an offer for a new Fox series titled *Glory Days*, created by a very talented writer-producer, Patrick Hasburgh. He had also created *21 Jump Street* and discovered Johnny Depp. *Glory Days* was about high school and college friends, recently graduated, starting their separate careers while trying to preserve their close friendships. The show was picked up for six episodes, and Patrick wanted me to direct two. The cast was young, talented and unknown. It filmed in Vancouver, Canada.

I accepted the job, and a few weeks later landed in the largest city in British Columbia, home of the Vancouver Canucks. I thought Vancouver was a stunning city, but my first day of filming was spent shooting outside scenes in a car that was being towed by an open camera truck with the crew and me on it. The film crew was extraordinary but the weather was horrible—freezing rain and hail. We toughed it out as we drove on slick streets getting pummeled by needle-sharp precipitation. The three actors we were filming did a good job, but they were a bit immature and not taking their work seriously enough. They also complained a lot about the cold, even though they (unlike the crew and I) had space heaters, blankets, and thermals. At the end of the day, the weather had gone through every layer of clothing that I had on; my skin and body were so numb that when I took a hot shower, I couldn't even feel the water. It was going to be a hell of a tough shoot.

The next day was cold, but happily the freezing rain and

hail had stopped. I had a few more outside scenes to direct at the Vancouver Zoo before we could all move inside to the studio. I arrived early and was getting some coffee when a young actor came up to me and said, "Hi, I'm Brad Pitt."

Brad and another actor were working that morning. Brad wanted to go over some ideas that he had for the scenes, including dialogue suggestions. It was obvious to me that Brad had spent a great deal of time working on his part and also studying the entire script. To say I was impressed is an understatement; I thought his suggestions were spot-on and not only improved his character, but other characters as well. While we were filming outside, he didn't ask for a coat between takes. He used the cold to add to the realness of the scene. Brad also had that X factor on camera—the kind that goes far beyond good looks and charisma. He had a God-given gift of connection.

As I mentioned before, the other cast members were good, but immature. They were not as prepared or committed as he was. What I found even more impressive was his heart. I noticed that Brad was always available (on the set or in his trailer) to talk to his colleagues, most of whom were insecure, and going through daily childish ups and downs. I knew he was calming them down and helping to relieve their anxieties. Not only did he help them, he also helped the show. A paying-it-forward type of guy. That is Brad Pitt.

The filming of both episodes went great. They were difficult shoots, but a lot of fun. On the last day of shooting we all said our goodbyes, but I didn't see Brad because he wasn't working that day. The next morning, I headed off to the airport for a flight home, hoping the show would do well. As I was checking in, I saw Brad hurrying to catch his own flight. He told me that he was on his way to screen test in Los Angeles for a film titled *Thelma and Louise*. I wished him "Good Luck" and off he went.

Glory Days was not picked up, but Brad landed the part that started his rise to—well, more than fame. I'm not surprised that he has become a super star and prolific producer, or that his *Twelve Years a Slave* won the Oscar for best picture. Even more so, I am not surprised that he is using his status to help people. Just like his talks with the cast on the *Glory Days* set, he continues to selflessly help people improve their lives. Only now he can help millions. The world is definitely a better place because of Brad Pitt.

"All dat matters is dey good dat goes on after you gone. Don't never forget dat, boy."

I will never forget, and don't worry, Willie, there are exceptional people, right now, making damn sure that the good goes on.

I Don't Have Time to Hold Back

"Be open to angels, let dem find you."

One Saturday afternoon, Willie was cleaning up around one of the checkouts, making a small girl laugh. She couldn't have been more than a year old and was being held by her mom. She was laughing so hard that her mom had to put her down to pay the bill. Willie continued to make funny faces and the child kept laughing. Suddenly, the girl started taking stilted steps toward Willie. Just before reaching him she started to fall, but Willie was able to catch her and pick her up.

"Oh my God!" the mom screamed, and rushed toward Willie.

Unnerved, Willie was frozen in place.

The mom bear hugged both of them. It turned out, this was the first time her daughter had walked. "You live on in dey hearts of all you touch. Dat way you never die, boy." Willie did more than say these words—he made sure that he touched hearts every day. When we worked together, whether it was sweeping down aisle five, dusting the furniture department, or waxing the appliance section's floor, he would look for places to connect. He taught me that the smallest things—making silly faces at a baby girl—could create moments between people that would last for a lifetime.

★ ★ ★

Happy Days was the number one show in the world, and I have to admit that the attention was overwhelming at times. All of us in the cast were constantly traveling, meeting people at high-adrenaline events, and basically not having a chance to plant our feet on the ground. A break from shooting was coming up when I received a call from the Cerebral Palsy National Organization. I had an ongoing relationship with them because of my volunteer work and my cousin, Annie. They sponsored a yearly camp in Florida for kids with CP during Easter week, and wanted to know if I'd be the celebrity camp counselor.

I was planning to go to Hawaii and relax, but decided it was more important to spend time with these kids and be part of something real. I said yes having no idea what my responsibilities would be when I got there. I knew the camp itself was not large, but it was beautiful. There were good-sized rustic cabins, a lodge where we could eat all of our meals, a swimming pool and other recreational facilities—all of it surrounded by expansive, vibrant, green land. There would be six kids in each cabin, and after a drawing, I would stay in the winning cabin.

I flew into Tampa and was met by Rick, a college-aged volunteer. He was studying to become a neurologist. He was a twin, and his brother had CP. Rick felt strongly about giving back and wanted to help find a cure for his brother. I learned that he was a terrific guy on our hour-long ride to the camp. When we arrived I was introduced to Jerry, who ran the camp. He showed me around before taking me to the cabin where I'd be residing. I met the boys, all between the ages of ten and twelve, all had CP, some more challenged than others. I was a bit confused. I was the only able-bodied person who would be staying in the cabin? I told Jerry that I didn't have experience in taking care of kids with CP.

"Don't worry, these kids take care of themselves. You are here for them to hang with and have fun."

Now, I admit I was really nervous. It was late in the day, and we needed to get ready for the dinner that would be served in the lodge, where I was to meet the rest of the counselors and campers. The cabin was equipped for persons with disabilities and had its own large bathroom with sinks, toilets, and showers. As the kids started to get ready, I watched as they helped each other. I saw the less-challenged helping the more-challenged. Not only that, they were having a blast together—they were 100 percent connected to the moment and each other. They didn't need my help to get ready for dinner. This was the beginning of my week of life lessons.

The lodge was built in the nineteenth century and all of its original wood floors and log walls were still in place. Jerry introduced me to the other counselors. I had already met Rick; the rest were equally impressive, all there to give from the heart. I was overwhelmed by everyone's pure commitment, campers included, and underwhelmed by my own character. Looking at all of the beaming faces that surrounded me, seeing the selflessness of everyone there, it occurred to me that I was the disabled one at this camp.

We were eating dinner when a woman in her twenties rushed in pushing a camper in his wheelchair. She had a smile that lit up the entire room. "Hi, Sunny!" the kids yelled as she escorted the young man to his table. Sunny, I guessed, was definitely the most popular counselor at the camp. And yes, that was her real name.

After we ate, the kids were allowed to play board games, watch cartoons screened from a 16 mm projector, listen to a story, read 'round a bonfire, or just sit on large, comfy couches and chairs and talk with their friends. I decided to listen to the story—*The Outsiders*. It was a clear evening and the sky was sparking with stars. About ten kids were huddled around the warm fire while Rick read the addictive words of S. E. Hinton.

"Hi there."

I turned.

"I wanted to introduce myself. I'm Sunny." Her angelic face, perfect features, blue eyes, and beach-blond hair brightened by the firelight made her seem like she belonged in a prince's palace, not a kid's camp in the wilderness.

"Want to go on a walk? I have a question to ask you."

Well, she was not only very beautiful, but also assertive. I'd never met anyone like her before.

I agreed to walk with her. After a few minutes it felt like we'd walked together many times before. She was a free spirit, connected to everything and everyone around her; being next to her opened my own heart. In fact, being with Sunny was like stepping outside of time and seeing things with new eyes, as if for the first time.

"I've never seen your show, but the kids have told me how much they love you, and now I can see why."

"How's that?" I answered.

She turned to me. "They feel needed because of you needing them. I watched you at dinner and by the fire. They're your teachers; they will help you to find you."

I was shocked silent. How could she possibly know what I was feeling?

"Now, here's my question," she said. "Will you let me hug you?"

Startled, I didn't know how to answer her. Sunny put her arms around me and gave me the most caring hug that I had ever experienced. All of my stress just faded away.

Sunny stepped back and took my hands in hers. Smiling, she looked at me for a few seconds and then finally said, "You know that we were destined to meet, Anson. You're a special person put on this earth to help people's lives, but you need your teachers to help you get there."

I didn't know what to say. Sunny sensed that and said, "When I feel the need to reach out to someone, I just do. I don't have time to hold back." She then gave me another hug and a tender kiss on the cheek before heading back to the camp, leaving me standing there speechless. Then she stopped and turned back. She smiled and without saying one word, planted her selfless love in my heart before continuing on.

"Did I just dream all of this?" I thought to myself. But I knew I didn't. I remembered Willie once saying, "You be open to angels, boy, let dem find you." An angel just came to me, I told myself. She touched my life forever. The lesson?

Get outside of myself; be in the moment, and be there for those that need me.

The next morning at breakfast, I didn't see Sunny, and I asked Jerry about her. He told me that she had been a volunteer for the past five years. At eighteen, she was on her way to a major career as a model when she learned that she had a rare form of breast cancer. It was terminal. They gave her five years with treatment just over four years ago. Ever since her prognosis, she'd dedicated her life to helping kids. She had left that morning for another round of chemo. Quickly, it all became clear, "I don't have time to hold back." My eyes began tearing up, and I told Jerry about my experience.

"That's Sunny," he said. "She lives her heart."

Less than two years later, Sunny passed on, but she lives in my heart; an angel who came into my life for one, brief shining moment, a moment that I pay forward every day.

"You live on in dey hearts of all you touch. Dat way you never die, boy."

LESSON 23

Big Al's

*"Someone look and say things too perfect . . . den
somethin' not perfect. Always looks inside, boy."*

Willie and I loathed the days when a new shipment of sofa
beds arrived at the store. We were the ones responsible for
getting them to the sales floor; they were heavy, twice the
weight of the average couch because of the bed frame and
mattress hidden inside. Exhausted after setting up the floor
samples one morning, Willie and I took a seat on one.

"Why doesn't a couch just have a mattress that folds out?"
I said to Willie, as the thought dawned on me. "Then you
wouldn't need a metal frame and the rest of the heavy stuff. It
would not only be lighter, but also cheaper."

Willie's face beamed, "You got God's gift, boy."

"What do you mean?"

"You see mo', make things better fo' everybody," Willie
replied. "You 'posed to move things forward. Dat's God's gift."

I wish I would have known how to move things forward

then . . . someone else invented the futon sixteen years later.

Willie saw something in me long before I did: I had a knack for finding things that could be improved and then creating solutions. He recognized my entrepreneurial destiny years before I did, and instilled the confidence I would later need to dream up new products and creative ways to sell them. He also taught me that I had a responsibility to use my "gift" to move the right products forward, products that contribute to people's lives. These gifts and lessons were paramount in pursuing my acting and musical careers. It was while I was doing *Happy Days* that I ventured outside of the entertainment industry and into my first product creation.

Al Molinaro, who played Al on the show and the owner of "Arnold's," was a talented comedic actor and a wonderful friend. He was also an entrepreneur and owned a very successful collection agency. He was looking for a new venture. About a year earlier, the *Happy Days* ball team played a charity game at Padres Stadium in San Diego. The owner of the team and stadium was Ray Kroc, the founder of McDonald's. Our charity game was a pregame before the Padres took the field, and then all of us were invited to watch the main game from Kroc's private box. I was able to speak with him about my entrepreneurial ambitions for a few minutes and he gave me a piece of invaluable advice: He said that the most important rule of selling a new product is how you sell it. You have to establish a connection to the consumer, and it might have nothing (or everything) to do with what you're selling. That's why he created characters (Ronald McDonald, Captain Crook, etc.) to sell his food; they were characters that people could fall in love with. Like Coke recreating Santa Claus to sell their drink.

I had an idea for a fast food business. I thought that if the food was fresh, and the restaurant sold nothing that had been frozen—well, it would give the consumer a healthier alternative to what was currently on the market. I spoke with Al about using his name. The world loved him and he was already known for hamburgers—would he want to open a place called "Big Al's"? He thought that it was a great idea, and that we wouldn't even have to license any rights, since "Al" was his legal name.

I was soon to learn one of the most frightening lessons of my life.

If you don't already know, let me tell you that having "gifts" is all well and good, but you also need the business education to back them up. I had a contact that knew executives at Coca-Cola who would put together a business pro-forma free of charge if we sold Coke exclusively in the restaurants. Al and I met with the Coke execs and they not only put together the business plan, but also set us up with a top-ranked fast food consultant. The consultant (who will remain nameless) was very excited about the whole concept; so excited that he convinced us to use our own money, partner with him, and get started.

Al and I were over the moon: Here was one of the most important people in the fast food business, who the giant Coca-Cola Company had recommended, and he wanted to be in business with us! The consultant's idea was to use Al's familiar face and place "Big Al's" restaurants in malls where there was not a McDonald's. We would build one, first, to see how it was received. Conveniently, there was a space available at a mall that was located right down from the consultant's offices, where he and his staff could oversee it.

Everything looked and sounded perfect. "Someone look and say things too perfect . . . den somethin' not perfect. Always looks inside, boy." I should have listened to Willie, because Al and I never did "look inside." The first Big Al's was a huge hit, so big a hit that a bank offered to finance nine more. Al and I could wait for our millions to arrive in sunny California while our partner's team did all of the work. How great was that? According to the consultant, all Al and I needed to do was show up at future openings and smile.

In a blink, we had ten successful restaurants. Or so we thought.

We weren't seeing any profits, but our partner told us that was because all of the money was going back into the business to pay off the loans quickly; he also convinced us to fund a franchise and Bam! We had ten more restaurants! In just over one year, Al and I were each one-third owners of a burgeoning twenty-restaurant chain. There was only one problem: We still hadn't seen a dime of profit. But what the heck, we were working with Coca-Cola and the best in the business. What could possibly go wrong?

If we had only done our due diligence, we would have known that our world-famous, highly-recommended consultant and partner not only had cash flow issues, but was also a functioning alcoholic, a prescription drug and gambling addict, and a true sociopath. He and his accountant were skimming all of the profits from our Big Al's locations to float his other restaurants and addictions.

One day Al and I received personal and business bankruptcy notices from our consultant's law firm. We found out that we were now both personally responsible for the day-today running of the restaurants, all the debt, the mall leases, and the franchise owners. Our days of waving from sunny California were over. We stood to lose our homes, our bank accounts, everything. We didn't know where to begin sorting out this disaster, and from where we were, things looked so far down they almost looked up. Luckily, we hired a wonderful guy who selflessly helped us clean up the terrible mess. We lost all of our investment, and our time spent—but not our lives.

I learned two large lessons from this experience: First, never be fooled by the image of anybody or anything—big companies, big titles, big offices, fancy cars, perfect clothes, pictures with Presidents, expensive restaurants—none of these things excuse you from performing due diligence. Second, never, ever go into a business without learning it and working it and taking on full responsibility for it. I've already mentioned that Willie taught me that sometimes you have to lose and hit rock bottom in order to climb back up. I did just that—and this time, I had the tools I needed to succeed, along with the wisdom and humility to stay on top. "Someone look and say things too perfect . . . den somethin' not perfect. Always looks inside, boy." I should have listened to you, Willie, but maybe, just maybe, I had to go through this tough lesson to grow up.

Show All of Them How Wrong They Are

"Age don't stop nothin'. Don't let nobody tell you different. Peoples tries to makes you feel like nothin', but you smarter and better. You keeps goin'. Never forget dat, boy."

After the Big Al's fiasco, I concentrated only on show biz for a while. I was directing comedy movies of the week for NBC, and I had an idea for a series of comedic films. My agent set up a meeting with the legendary Aaron Spelling, the most successful producer in television history. It would take place at his beautiful home. To say that I was nervous was an understatement.

Upon arrival, I was led into a large, exquisitely decorated living room and offered refreshments by a formal white-jacketed waiter. He brought me coffee on a silver tray with freshly baked scones. Just as I was taking a bite I heard, "So sorry I'm late, Anson. I had a phone call that took longer than expected."

There stood Aaron Spelling in person, and he was not what I expected. He was warm, humble, and gracious, and immediately made me feel comfortable; the same feeling that I had when I met President Reagan. We discussed my idea and he loved it. He offered me a development contract with his company on the spot. As I walked out his front door toward my car, I couldn't believe how lucky I was and thought, "Wow! I'm in business with Aaron Spelling!"

A few weeks later, I drove onto the Warner Hollywood Studio lot, formerly Samuel Goldwyn Studios, and before that Pickford-Fairbanks Studios. This is where Aaron had his company's headquarters, and it was my first day with Spelling Productions. The head of facilities took me to my bungalow office, a beautiful, retro building with years of history attached to it—I was told that Mary Pickford used it as her private office in the twenties. Walking into my new digs, I thought, Hey Willie, wish we could set up the oil drum cans in here. Would be a great "Dey Talk" room. I was then taken over to a warehouse where hundreds of pieces of set furniture, etc., were stored. I was told to pick a desk, couch, chairs, pictures— whatever I needed—to furnish the office. All of it was brought over and set up by the end of the day. Before I left, I got word that Aaron wanted to see me at ten the next morning.

Aaron had exquisite taste; actually his wife, Candy, had exquisite taste. She really knew how to make things beautiful. Walking into his enormous office was jaw-dropping. There had to be at least four large seating areas and a full bar, with a bartender and full-time waiter. Again, I was served coffee on a silver tray. Aaron wanted me to put together a presentation for a meeting with his agency, Creative Artists (CAA).

It would take place at the end of the week. He said that they would be quite helpful in bringing in writers and star talent for my projects.

The meeting was intimidating; there were at least six agents in the room, along with Aaron's creative staff. I thought that I did a good job presenting my wares, but I could feel a lack of excitement. After I was finished, Aaron asked me to leave; he said that they had other business to discuss. I was putting my materials back in my briefcase, just outside Aaron's closed door, when I heard Aaron saying something about them not doing anything—that they were just making money on past shows. He didn't sound happy. I finished organizing my stuff and headed back to my office. A few hours later, I again got a call asking me to come and see Aaron.

This time when I entered his office he was sitting alone, no bartender or waiter. He motioned for me to walk over and sit down. I could tell that something was bothering him, and I hoped that it wasn't me. He told me that I did a great job in the meeting. The problem was between him and his agency. Even though CAA continued to make millions on his film library, the company (and all of Hollywood for that matter) thought that he was through, that he was a dinosaur and should just fade away.

I recalled something I'd heard Willie say many years before. "Age don't stop nothin'. Don't let nobody tell you different. Peoples tries to makes you feel like nothin', but you smarter and better. You keeps goin'. Never forget dat, boy." Willie hated when older people were not given chances— were basically put out to pasture. He felt that it was as much a form of prejudice as racism: "Just damn wrong."

Aaron's next words inspired me then (and to this day). "I'm sixty-five years old," he said, "and I still have the fire in my gut. I'm going to do it one more time. I'm going to show all of them how wrong they are."

Here was the most successful television producer in history having to prove his worth all over again; a courageous, talented man, who had the guts to march to his own drummer and start again, and the rest be damned! I felt honored that Aaron shared his feelings and goals with me.

And boy, did he do it again! *Beverly Hills 90210, Melrose Place*, and *Charmed* are just a few of the hit shows he created his "second time around."

Aaron Spelling was as loyal as he was talented, and he kept me working on many of his shows. His continued success and inspiration also gave me the guts to start a totally unexpected career: creating a multi-million dollar product company at the age of fifty.

"Age don't stop nothin'. Don't let nobody tell you different."

Melrose Place and StarMaker

*"Good opportunities suppo' to happen if you stand still
and let it show itself."*

Aaron Spelling was hotter then he'd ever been, making the entire Hollywood industry eat crow. He was also very generous, contracting me to direct many of his new shows. My favorite was *Melrose Place,* one of the most popular shows in the world and a lot of fun to work on. The entire cast was great and so was the creative team.

One morning, the cast members were raving about a skin treatment they'd received in the make-up trailer that had crushed pearls in it. Crushed pearls, I thought, my interest piqued. The actors couldn't stop talking about it, and my instincts said to investigate. So during a lighting set-up, I visited the make-up trailer and met JoAnna Connell. She was a top make-up artist (Madonna and Tom Cruise were her clients) and also a skin care specialist. She had created all of the skin and self-tanning treatments used on the original *Baywatch* series. Numerous movies and television shows brought her in to do skin treatments on stars. When I met her, she was showing the *Melrose* make-up department her crushed pearl treatment. I asked her if her products were in stores. She said that they were not, that she and her chemist made bulk batches only for shows that requested it.

Now, one day in "Dey Talk Room," after he heard a radio commercial about getting rich quick, Willie shook his head in disagreement. "Don't believe no get rich commercial and runs after it. Den you don't lead, and greedy peoples lead you." He told me that "good opportunities are suppo' to happen if you stand still and let it show itself." Standing in that make-up trailer, his voice roared in my head! I was looking at a woman who created real, working beauty products that were used daily on the most famous faces in the world. What if the public could buy these exact products? Talk about "good opportunities are suppo' to happen if you stand still and let it show itself"! Nothing else like JoAnna Connell's treatments was on the market.

I was fifty years old. I knew nothing about the beauty business (let alone manufacturing, legalities, commerce) and I'd had that near-disaster with Big Al's . . . and yet instead of walking away, I thought about Aaron Spelling, and the fire in his gut. It was exactly what I was feeling. JoAnna knew a lot about beauty and I could see she felt that same fire. So we became partners, and together we created StarMaker Products. The crushed pearl skin care treatment became our first product for sale (and was successful on QVC for a decade). I branded it "Micro Pearl Abrasion."

Unlike with Big Al's, this time I was determined to do

things right, and JoAnna made it a lot easier. She was a great businesswoman, and fiscally conservative. We first secured commitments for packaged versions of our products from television shows that knew about her; this way we were never in the red. We had buyers for our wares before they were even produced. Then, through trial and error, we began to manufacture small runs for our film industry commitments. We knew we were a long way from becoming a consumer brand in the marketplace, and that we still had a hell of a lot to learn.

While we were nurturing StarMaker Products, I was directing a lot of Spelling shows. Aaron was not in the best health, and he now left the day-to-day responsibilities of his company to a new executive who, unbeknownst to Aaron, had his own agenda. One of his goals was to get rid of Aaron's people in a clever and politically correct way.

I was directing the show *Charmed* at a warehouse in Woodland Hills. Across the street was the Woodland Hills Swap Meet, the largest of its kind in Southern California. JoAnna and I needed to obtain consumer research for StarMaker Products, but the market research companies we had contacted were demanding over $200,000 to do the job. Ten thousand people walked through the swap meet every weekend. Why couldn't that be our market research?

We set up a meeting and found that we could rent a space at the Swap Meet for only $400 a month. We would have access to thousands of people, each and every weekend, who could sample our product, write opinions, and give us their contact information. In other words, we could get everything we needed from the market research companies for only $4800 a year plus product cost. What a deal! And what a way to make sure the responsibility of our fledgling company would stay in our own hands: We would be the labor. JoAnna and I rented a space and started to get everything ready.

The very next week, after finishing up an episode of *Charmed,* I was told to go to the production office. The episode was brought in under budget, so I thought that I was going to get an "Atta Boy!" Instead I got an "Outta here!" I would not be directing any more episodes. I was now persona non grata on other Spelling shows as well. In three words, I was out.

"Dey times things need to be so bad to be so good. Gotta drop to da bottom to find da way." Willie's lesson came roaring back. I had to suck up my ego, forget the unfairness of my situation, use my energies to move forward with StarMaker, and launch a brand new career. JoAnna and I set up shop at the swap meet as planned, and we worked it together every Friday through Sunday for almost a year. As we had hoped, thousands of consumers tried our products, and we were able to accumulate valuable information for the building of our company.

"Can you believe he's here?" I heard one Friday at lunchtime. "He must be really bad off. It's embarrassing."

I looked up, and across the aisle from the booth were some members of the *Charmed* crew, watching me. They had no idea that I was launching a new business. They saw their former director selling stuff at a swap meet and judged me as a loser. It was ironic, then, when less than two years later they all began calling me. They'd found out that StarMaker Products were selling all over the world and now saw me as a winner and their new inspiration. They wanted to know how to launch their own products. They wanted to know what magic I had found to turn my life around . . . The magic was one more teacher.

QVC? It's Impossible to Get On There

"Sometime de little person is de big person.
Don't never judge, boy."

A customer at the store realized that she underpaid for her purchases after she got to her car and saw that certain items weren't rung up on her receipt. Having been a cashier herself once, she knew that the worker could get in trouble for the mistake. So she walked back into Leonard's with the items, brought it to the attention of the cashier, and then paid for them. She was right: The worker would have gotten in trouble. Willie said, "Dere's doz people dat don't let nobody or nothin' change dere good self. Dey always do da right thing. Never let go of dem, boy, dey God's hand."

Unfortunately, these kinds of individuals are rare in today's world; too many greedy people are out for themselves no matter what the cost. JoAnna and I found this to be especially true in the product business—make that the entire world of commerce. We were working hard at the swap meet and I was still reeling since my fall from grace as a director, but I knew that I had to keep moving forward. We were still using our chemist and her workers to hand-fill limited industry orders, but our goal was to finish our market research and then—in the future—sell to the general public. At this point, if we did sell thousands of units we'd be in nothing but trouble. Neither JoAnna nor I knew the first thing about mass production yet, or the huge responsibilities and commitments that go along with it.

Well . . . one day, a friend set up an appointment for us with someone who specialized in direct-mail sales. We really didn't think that could possibly work for us, but something deep inside pushed us forward and we took the meeting. What we didn't know was that the person we were meeting with, Jeff Giordano, was also one of the major players in direct-response television, which included the largest home shopping network in the world, QVC. At the meeting we all quickly agreed that our products were not right for direct mail, but Jeff was quite intrigued with Micro Pearl Abrasion.

As JoAnna and I were heading back to the car after the meeting, my cell phone rang. "Hey, this is Jeff. Have you ever thought about QVC?"

"I heard that it's impossible to get on there," I replied.

"I need to know if you're interested," he said.

"I just don't want to waste time," I answered.

"Do you want to get the hell on or not?" Jeff retorted.

"Sure," I countered. I was thinking, what a dreamer.

"I'll get back to you," and he hung up.

Days later we not only knew about the relationship Jeff had with QVC—we had also sold QVC 6,500 units of Micro

Pearl Abrasion to a very special person and talented buyer, Bernadette Voelker. It was a dream that almost turned into a nightmare.

It turns out that when you sell to a giant like QVC there are numerous requirements you must fulfill: everything from safety tests to specific packaging, pack-outs, delivery schedules, and on and on. We were newbies and it was overwhelming. JoAnna and I had only a few weeks to have all of the completed samples, clinical testing, paperwork, pricing, etc., done and on our QVC buyer's desk. If not, we'd lose this once-in-a-lifetime opportunity. We didn't even have a manufacturing facility that could perfect the formula and create such large numbers of units!

JoAnna and I asked people for help, but we asked the wrong people. They were individuals that Willie would have called "de users" and companies who didn't want to help as much as they wanted to take advantage of us. Days went by, and it looked like we were going to fail. We were getting frustrated and panicky; I was having a hard time sleeping, it got so bad.

As the deadline loomed (and after finally falling asleep), I had a dream. Willie and I were in "Dey Talk Room," and he was telling me, "Sometime de little person is de big person. Don't never judge, boy." I instantly woke up and had the answer to our problems: JoAnna and I knew a product-packaging salesman! His name was Lonnie Stephan, and he worked with numerous manufacturing labs in Southern California.

We took Lonnie out to lunch and sure enough, he had all of the information that we needed to complete QVC's requirements. He recommended a lab, Cosmetic Technologies in Newbury Park, California. Lonnie set everything in motion for us. One good-hearted salesman who cared moved us forward—not a large corporation or an expensive consultant. "Sometime de little person is de big person. Don't never judge, boy." This is probably the most important lesson Willie ever taught me.

We called the owner of Cosmetic Technologies, Ron Lewis, and explained our situation and our deadline. He was amazing—he cleared his calendar so that he could meet with us the next morning.

"Dere's doz people dat don't let nobody or nothin' change dere good self. Dey always do da right thing. Never let go of dem, boy, dey God's hand." Ron Lewis was "doz people": an extraordinary, brilliant, talented, and ethical man. He took us under his wing and mentored us. He not only manufactured (and perfected) our first QVC product, but he was also instrumental in making sure that every detail—clinical testing, packaging, labeling, everything—was done one hundred percent correctly.

Ron taught us the product business because he believed, like Willie, that we should use our talents to create good things that contribute to and improve people's lives. Without him, JoAnna and I might still be at the swap meet hoping and praying that another break like the QVC one we messed up would come along. He selflessly educated us, and made damn sure that we were a success and built a successful company.

Today, StarMaker has manufactured over forty products: everything from beauty creams to disposable lint remover sheets. It's a fantastic feeling to know that lives have been improved because of a company that would have never gotten off the ground without Lonnie Stephan, the packaging salesman, and Ron Lewis, a teacher using both of God's hands. He taught JoAnna and me the product business—and more importantly, he helped me become a better man. And if you were wondering: We sold out on our first QVC show. It was the start of StarMaker Product's national success.

Heart of Light

"Some people's got God's glow.
Dey healers dat heal hearts."

An older gentleman with a disability, Ben, would occasionally buy things at Leonard's. He walked with two canes, never stopped smiling, and insisted that he do things himself. What was amazing about him was the beacon of light that he radiated—almost like heaven's follow-spot was continuously tracking him. Ben literally brightened up the aisles he walked down, and all of the people that he met. When you talked with him, you could actually feel his positive energy, and it made the rest of your day better. Ben loved Willie, who had his own shining light, and would sometimes bring Willie a sandwich from Lancer's—the restaurant that shared the same parking lot as the store. They would sit outside and eat together, making a bright, beautiful day even brighter. Willie said of Ben, "Some people's got God's glow. Dey healers dat heal hearts."

★ ★ ★

I first saw Dolly Parton on the Porter Wagner television show in the very early seventies. I was not a country music fan because I was never really exposed to it. One night I was over at my friend's house and his dad—he was from Tennessee and a country music fanatic—called us in to watch *The Porter Wagoner Show*. I saw a girl who was pretty, but a little over the top with her hair and make-up. Then she performed a song that she had written titled "Coat of Many Colors." I became an instant fan. Her music went beyond country for me—it went right to my heart.

Dolly Parton started breaking out on her own during the first years of *Happy Days*. In 1976 I received a call from my agent who told me that Dolly had a new syndicated variety show; they wanted me as a guest. I was very excited and couldn't say yes fast enough. Then the day before I flew down to Nashville to tape the show, I came down with a sore throat. I was feeling pretty badly when I got off of the plane. I was driven straight to a rehearsal where I met Dolly for the first time. She gave me the warmest hug and when she heard my voice, she instantly knew that I didn't feel well.

"You just stay in your dressing room and rest yourself," she told me. As she walked away I noticed her light, the kind that followed Ben. "Some people's got God's glow." I was taken to my dressing room, but before I even walked in I started feeling better.

A bit later, a production assistant came by to tell me that they were sorry for the delay; Dolly had something come up. Well, what came up turned out to be me. This wonderful woman had gotten me some throat spray. She also made sure that I had hot herbal tea. I had never met a more giving performer, ever. No wonder her songs and her charm touch the world, I thought. She is more than the heart of music, she is the heart of light: someone who dreams big and cares more.

We rehearsed and shot the show the next day. Maybe it was the throat spray or maybe the tea, but I really think that it was the magic of Dolly Parton that made me feel great. It turned out that she did the same for her crew and friends, whoever needed her help. Talking with the people that worked with her, I was astounded to learn about the selfless, quiet help that Dolly gave them, from monetary assistance to emotional healing. This gallant woman not only wrote songs about the need for human connection—she damn well gave it.

Through the years, I've read a lot of articles about Dolly, but not enough of them touch on the person that she really is, and that is why I've included this story. Not long after I guested on her show, she recorded and released the most popular song of her career to date: a song that crossed over to the pop charts and made her a mega-star, "Here You Come Again." In a blink, Dolly was known to the world as both a country artist and a pop star. I was thrilled for her success. A few months later, my agent received a request for me to be a presenter at the American Music Awards, airing on ABC. I accepted and was excited to be included. It turned out that my co-presenter would be Dolly Parton, who was now well on her way to becoming a superstar.

The afternoon of the show there was a rehearsal (yes, even the award presenters rehearse). When I met Dolly again, nothing had changed. She had the exact same warmth and heart. In fact, one of the stagehands had a cold, and there was

Dolly finding him Kleenex. Again I realized that I was working with a talented woman who dreamed big, but cared more. That night we presented two awards and believe me, Dolly didn't need a spotlight, God's light follows her every path.

"Some people's got God's glow. Dey healers dat heal hearts."

I wish that you could have met her, Willie. You, Ben, and Dolly would have had a sandwich outside together, brightening and healing the world.

Strength of Character

*"He be my leader. Lead me to dey right places in my
head. He always see dey good in me and make it better."*

One chilly and rainy Saturday there was a lull in business
at the store. I finished cleaning up the entrance area and
then looked for Willie. I found him talking with a kind-
looking older gentleman near the office area. Willie looked
different . . . younger . . . reminding me of a small child, his
face beaming, as he listened intently. Usually it was the other
way around—Willie talking while others listened. After a
few minutes the two exchanged a warm hug and then the
gentleman departed.

Back in "Dey Talk Room," I asked Willie who the man
was. He said, "He be my leader. Lead me to dey right places in
my head. He always see dey good in me and make it better."

It turned out that he was a minister. Willie first met him
years earlier while delivering furniture to his church. Ever
since then, the minister would occasionally drop by the store

to check up on him. What Willie liked was that this minister never judged or tried to change him; he accepted him for who he was. Willie said, "Dey man knows dat only change come from wanting to. He make it so you want to." He added that these leaders are "important" and you "needs to watch dem and listen."

I've been lucky enough to watch and listen to a man like this for almost forty years and counting. Ron Howard is a man of great character—one of the purest individuals that I've met since Willie. Yes, he's tremendously talented, and yes, he's extremely successful, but most importantly, he's a selfless leader "dat always see dey good in me and make it better." From the first moment we met, Ron has had a quiet maturity way beyond his years. He never got too high or too low; he was always even keel. His work ethic was impeccable and he never, ever let his ego rule. It was always the work first and himself second, or even third. A good example is when he took a back seat to Henry Winkler on *Happy Days*. Henry's character, Fonzie, had skyrocketed in popularity, and the network wanted to put him up front in the show. Ron had a strong contract and could have easily said no, but he knew what was best for the show's success and quickly agreed to take a back seat.

Every day we worked together, Ron quietly made me a better person. I would observe his actions; I would watch him actively making everybody around him feel good and positive. I knew that he would never further himself by hurting somebody else; he had the strength of character to get ahead by always doing the right thing.

Ron earned his directing success through hard work. In

fact, most people don't know that Ron won a national Kodak Film contest when he was only twelve years old. He won for best 8 mm film that was cut in the camera, meaning that there was no editing. Each shot was designed to fit perfectly with the following and so on. He did this at twelve years old! Ron won this award on pure talent—he entered by mail along with thousands of other contestants.

For years, he tried to gain a foothold directing, but nobody would give him a chance. Still, I never heard him say a bad word about anyone. He only worked harder and got better. It was Ron who convinced me that I had the talent to produce and create television shows, and it was Ron who gave me the opportunity to succeed. Together we had meetings at NBC and ABC to sell my first shows. After he started making hit films, like *Splash*, he agreed to back me up on my first directing gig. (You remember I told you earlier: if I screwed up, he would come in and take over. This made the network comfortable working with me, a first time director.) What was really incredible about Ron's gesture was that at the time he was a huge feature director, yet he was willing to back me up on an ABC *Afterschool Special*. That was simply unheard of; but that's Ron, a friend who is always there for you, and a leader who sees the best in you.

Ron is now one of the most successful individuals in the industry; not only as a director, but also as a film and television producer, and the owner of the prolific Imagine Entertainment. He's also raised a wonderful family, and has given back so much to so many. You don't hear about his generosity because he never mentions it . . . he does it from his heart. He transcends the magical movies he makes with the magic he unselfishly gives to others. He's a rare individual in today's gluttonous world, a man who made it the right way and has given back even more.

"He be my leader. Lead me to dey right places in my head. He always see dey good in me and make it better."

LESSON 29

A Wealth of Positive Energy

"Der's no age for answers.
God's help come from all ages."

Willie once told me that he received important help and advice from a fifteen-year-old boy, advice that saved and turned his life around. Willie was in his thirties at the time and homeless, living on the streets of some city that he must have mentioned, but that I've long ago forgotten. Leaving home at sixteen years old, neither loved nor educated, he was a broken man: drinking his pain numb and panhandling for survival. One chilled winter day while sitting on the sidewalk, turned from the street to shield himself from the bitter cold, cheap booze in his hands, he felt a warm blanket placed on his shoulders. Turning around, he saw a young boy, probably fifteen years old, with blankets in hand. The boy gave him another one for his legs. Willie was touched by the boy's gifts, but even more so by the kindness in his young eyes. He told me, "He had dey light of God in doz eyes."

The boy was a volunteer for a rescue mission, and had gotten a bunch of his high school friends to join with him. This kid was the first person in a very long time to break through Willie's anger and deadness, bringing him food and fellowship on subsequent days, and good feelings back into his life. Willie told me that the boy told him, "What you wants in your life, you needs to give to someone else. If I wants to feel betta, den I gots to make someone else feel betta." He gazed at me for a long moment, and then finally said, "Dat's why I give back to you, boy. I gives to me too."

The young man gave Willie hope and purpose, and finally convinced him that he deserved to let the mission help him to get back on his feet. It wasn't long before Willie started his life again. "Der's no age for answers boy, God's help come from all ages."

In the years ahead, I was destined to learn the same lesson.

StarMaker Products was doing great, but it had been a while since I directed a television show. One afternoon, out of the blue, I got a call from my agent with an offer to direct one segment of a new series called *The Secret Life of the American Teenager*. It was about a pregnant teenager and the responsibilities that come with being a mom in high school. It was the first show to deal honestly with the reality of unprotected teenage sex. Well, what started as one episode turned into a five-year job directing a third of the shows. The cast and crew were fantastic, but the standout was a sixteen-year-old actress named Shailene Woodley. She played the young pregnant girl who becomes a single mom. I first heard of Shailene from my friend Don Most, who played Ralph on *Happy Days*. He had directed Shailene in a terrific film called *Moola*. Don is a very talented director, and he had nothing but raves for Shailene—he praised her professionalism and lack of ego at such a young age. He said her talent and integrity reminded him of a young Ron Howard.

On my first day working with Shailene, her talent and work ethic were not the only things that astounded me—I was also bowled over by her kind heart. She radiated a wealth of positive energy to the entire cast and crew. I could see that she cared much more about all those around her than she did about herself. Like Don, she reminded me of Ron Howard, but also of Dolly Parton. Even after the show became the most popular in the ABC Family network's history, she had the integrity to stay who she was and maintain her innate understanding of the importance of balance and nature.

Shailene cares about the planet that we all share, and she takes personal responsibility to keep it (and us all) healthy. She has a huge appreciation for life, and uses her high profile to educate and make people's lives better—she is not the kind of person who wants to sell a profitable clothing or make-up line. Instead she is an enlightened young lady who walks the walk. She grows and cooks her own food and hikes to a special stream to fill containers with her week's water. She knows every edible and inedible plant on earth, what foods to eat and stay away from and why, how to keep herself in the best health, and on and on. I worked with Shailene from the time she was sixteen to the time she was twenty years old, and I really believe that she helped me grow more than I helped her.

"Der's no age for answers, boy, God's help come from all ages." You were right, Willie. I'd never imagined that my life would be transformed by a sixteen-year-old. Then again, who would have thought it possible that a fifteen-year-old could have saved yours? And that you, in turn, would make this impossible story possible?

Shailene educated and inspired me. She taught me how to make a healthier, happier world. I asked her once, "Who are the people that impress you?" and she answered, "People that make a difference."

Shailene Woodley is making a vast difference. She moves the world with her artistic talent and improves the world with her heart. She marches to her own drummer with "Dey light of God in doz eyes."

LESSON 30

A Conversation with Willie

"I always be with you, boy."

Waking up this morning, I had an overpowering need to see Willie. It's kind of crazy—I mean, it's been over forty years since we last spoke—still, I got in my car and drove to Leonard's Department Store. Walking in, the place looked exactly the same. I went to the back and the door of "Dey Talk Room" was open. Looking in, it hadn't changed either: the same rusted oil drum cans, age-stained walls, and smell of Marlboros and whiskey in the air. Willie was standing by his makeshift desk, finishing up a smoke.

WILLIE: Sit yerself down, boy.

Feeling fifteen again, I do as I'm told. Willie puts out his cig and sits on the drum next to me.

WILLIE: . . . You lookin' fine.

    ME: You're looking good too, Willie.

Willie hasn't aged at all.

WILLIE: So, tell me yer story, boy.

Tell my story? It's been decades since we last talked. Willie sensed that I didn't even know where to start.

WILLIE: (*Smiling*) . . . Need to know if it be
              happy.

He didn't want my life story. He just wanted to know that I was okay.

    ME: Yeah, everything's great. How are you
           doing?

WILLIE: I be good. (*Laughing*) Gots me enough
           whiskey to stops the bad.

You see, Willie never stopped drinking, but he learned how to control it. He went through so much pain in his life that it could never go away, not completely, and sometimes he just needed a little help to keep on going.

WILLIE: You workin' hard, boy? Got yerself a
           family?

ME: Yeah, been working steady. Have a great
family: five kids, Willie . . . all girls.

WILLIE: You a blessed man, dey always takes care
of der daddy."

ME: Yeah, if they don't kill you first.

WILLIE: (*Laughing*) Yeah, boy, dey can do dat too.

He takes his flask out of his pants pocket and gets a taste.

ME: I needed to see you and thank you.

WILLIE: For what, boy?

How do you say everything? I guess you just say. . .

ME: Everything.

WILLIE: (*Laughing out loud*) Dat's a big word, boy.

ME: Well, you gave me a big life, Willie . . .
(*Getting emotional*) . . . and I never got
the chance to tell you that.

WILLIE: (*Confused*) What I do?

ME: You talked to me.

WILLIE: (*Laughs*) I talks to everbody.

ME: Before I met you, everyone talked at me.
You were the first that talked to me.

WILLIE: (*Touched*) Dat's kind, boy.

ME: You made sure that I found myself . . .
(*Wiping away tears*) . . . and you made sure
that you were with me every day since.

Willie smiles, lighting up the room, and puts his hand on my shoulder.

WILLIE: You be wit me too, boy.

ME: I don't understand.

WILLIE: You takes wit you what you give. We talks 'bout dat before.

ME: (*Remembering*) . . . Yeah, we did.

WILLIE: Well . . . Gots to be goin, boy. Promise dey furniture man dat I shine his floor up. He say dey sell lots better dat way.

He goes over and gets his floor waxer.

ME: . . . But I just got here.

Willie puts down the waxer and walks up to me.

WILLIE: . . . We talks enough. Good to see you and good to know dat everthin's movin' on. Dat's what it all about, boy.

ME: There's so much you don't know. So much has happened.

WILLIE: Knows enough, and I is proud of you, boy, but dey talks are done now. You gots five daughters and lots of peoples dat needs you. It's der turn.

He takes a step closer.

WILLIE: You gots me with you . . . no needs to go
          back. You and me be movin' on.

He gives me a hug that makes everything feel right.

WILLIE: I loves you, boy.
ME: I love you too, Willie.

He and his waxer then start out the door. Just outside, he
turns to me one last time.

WILLIE: I always be with you, boy.

It's then that I woke up . . .

And it all became suddenly clear. I needed to pay Willie's
wisdom forward so that everyone can have their talks in "Dey
Talk Room," so that everyone has that chance to find themselves and move on. That's the reason for this book, to inspire
you to stop looking at your mountain and to start climbing it,
just like Willie did for me . . . 'Cause you knows what?

"You gonna do somethin' great in life. Just a feelin' I got."

Epilogue

Singing to a Bulldog would never have been written if it weren't for Dr. Roberta Temes's book *How to Write a Memoir in 30 Days*. For years, people have been saying to me that I should write a book about my life; for even longer, I have wanted to share with the world Willie Turner's lessons and the profound effect he had on who I became as an individual, giving me the tools for a full-bodied life.

I always thought, "Someday, when I have more time, I'll write that book." Then a friend gave me a copy of Dr. Temes's book and I was inspired to start immediately. It not only gave me a detailed, step-by-step guide to write my first memoir, but also the confidence that I could do it successfully. I encourage you to make the time to tell your story.

How to Write a Memoir in 30 Days

Step-by-Step Instructions for Creating and Publishing Your Personal Story

Roberta Temes, Ph.D

Reader's digest

The Reader's Digest Association, Inc.
New York, NY • Montreal

Introduction

The book that's been rattling around in your head is ready to reveal itself.

Simply follow the daily directions and by next month you will have a memoir ready to submit for publishing.

Just write what you are asked to write for each day's assignment and your memoir will appear. You might decide to do this entirely on your computer, or you might print it out and keep your pages in a folder or you might handwrite it all in a notebook. If you prefer not to write, then speak into a recorder (perhaps your phone can record?) and when you complete the thirty assignments you will have an audio book. If you then wish to turn it into a written book, all you need to do is find a transcriptionist who will type out your recorded words.

Congratulations for undertaking this project. Your memoir will let the world know just who you are and what you've been through all these years. Whether you're writing so that colleagues will know your professional story, or so that relatives will know the truth about your family story, your memoir is important. They may not yet realize it, but your children and their children and grandchildren may one day want to know about you—your opinions, your ideas. The general public may appreciate your story, too. An interesting story is worth telling. It is wise to leave a written or oral legacy. Learning about your life—your milestones as well as your struggles—is instructive and useful, and it can be entertaining, too. All your readers can learn from you—they can learn about hopes and about happiness, and perhaps unhappiness, too. How did you do it? How did you get this far? You can be an inspiration, or a warning, depending upon your life story.

Tell them. Teach them. What were the major conflicts of your life? How did you resolve those conflicts? Do you still resolve conflicts that way? Were the conflicts with other people? Were the conflicts within yourself? The writing assignments you do will clarify all these situations.

As you delve into your past, you will notice certain themes and patterns that continue to show up in your life. Recalling some old, formerly-forgotten memories will help you make sense out of your life and increase your understanding of yourself. You will give a voice to your desires, disappointments, and accomplishments too.

Releasing repressed emotions helps you mature emotionally; often when you write about past events, buried emotions come into your mind. Writing your memoir has some neurological value too. It stimulates your memory and thus increases your cognitive functioning. Studies have shown that when people write about personal thoughts for as few as ten minutes each day, they have an easier time falling asleep and staying asleep throughout the night. Writing about negative life events frees your mind from secretly storing those memories, and you will notice that you'll have more available energy. When your writing allows you to re-experience positive life events, you boost your happiness level. When you let your true self be known, you invite others to appreciate you.

After you complete each daily assignment, simply save it. Later on, you'll be instructed in techniques that will merge all your daily writings into one memoir. If you wish to include material from a blog or personal journal, that, too, will be merged.

You are in charge of figuring out how quickly you complete your memoir. I hope you will find time to write every day; that maintains your momentum and you truly will finish in one month. Some people set their alarm for one hour earlier than usual and write every morning, and then finish the assignment at the end of the day. Of course, if you are able to work on your memoir only on the weekends, or perhaps only three days a week, the program will still work for you. No matter how you choose to do this, you will have a completed memoir at the end of 30 writing sessions.

Many writers prefer a specific writing place—a desk in the bedroom, a particular table at the local coffee shop, a special chair in the living room. A designated writing area is a good idea because your brain will immediately associate your writing spot with actual writing, and extraneous thoughts will stay away. You won't be tempted to think of other things when you sit down to write.

Please write about yourself with enthusiasm and with honor. Your memoir is a story and you are the main character—you are the hero. In a literary work, the main character is referred to as the protagonist. This is your life and you are in charge of how you present it. It's time to tell your story.

Day 1

Think about your life and then sum it up in two or three sentences. Don't rush; let your mind wander in all directions. You may focus on particular years or precise points of your life, or you may choose to encompass a wide range of experiences.

Here are some examples of two- and three-sentence summaries:

I was blessed with good genes. I've had good luck. There are no regrets.

Pathetic life. My dog is my best friend.

Please don't be scared of me. I have schizophrenia. I would never hurt anyone.

I'm lucky because I always sleep well. But I've been unlucky because I never work well. I've had lots of job problems.

My uncle ruined my life. He molested me not once, but twice. And I let him.

I definitely married the wrong man. I have great kids. He doesn't see them, thank God.

My son wants to kill me. This is the truth.

I sell real estate. It is a big bore. I know I should look for a new job, but I can't get started.

My whole life I have messed up. My whole life she has gotten me out of messes. I wonder every day if I could change.

My mom was always sick. My dad bolted. My childhood was lousy.

Dance, aerobics, tennis, and yoga. That's my life.

People don't know that I am lonely and sad. That's because I am rich and handsome. People are easily fooled.

I love to read. I love to work. Life is great.

My childhood was traumatic. My teen years were terrible. Finally, I am happy now.

Religion saved me and now I want to spread the word. Before my awakening, I was nasty.

I'm lonely. But maybe it's my fault because I don't like anybody.

I am obedient to a fault. I have always been like that.

Life was hard for my parents but easy for me. Good education, good jobs, great family. I am blessed.

Now it's your turn. You might write and rewrite; that's okay. Think about your life and permit all your memories to rise up in your mind. Pondering to produce your sentences stimulates your memory and makes it easier for you to recall your early years and the significant events of your life.

Day 2

A memoir is not an autobiography. An autobiography is strictly factual and chronologically covers your life from birth until today. It is accurate and full of facts and explanations. Whereas an autobiography states facts, a memoir describes your reactions to those facts. For example, an autobiography might discuss social and political ideas of the times, but your memoir would discuss your emotional responses to those ideas. Your autobiography is a photograph, a picture showing precise detail. Your memoir, on the other hand, is an impressionistic painting—a canvas conveying a general impression using free brushstrokes to create a general feeling.

Memoirs are emotional reminiscences. Your memoir is your account of how you remember certain experiences. It's only as accurate as your memory permits and that's just fine. It's more important that you accurately portray your emotions than accurately list the facts. It's okay to approximate dialogue and it's okay to present events out of order. It is not okay to create imaginary events and imaginary characters, but enhancing what already exists is occasionally appropriate.

In your memoir, you will talk about and describe certain memories, figuring out why they are important. You'll investigate how and why particular incidents influenced your life.

Don't give in to the temptation to simply present your life, one year at a time, as an autobiographical report. Your memoir will cover only a few select years, or only a few select issues. Sometimes a memoir discusses only one aspect of your life, and sometimes a memoir is about a consistent theme that runs throughout your life.

There are memoirs about high school years, about years devoted to bringing up babies, about years of caring for a sick relative. There are memoirs about a lifelong relationship with a beloved teacher, with a mentally ill parent, with a family pet. You might write a memoir about your trip to France or about your search for a long-lost relative or about your years as a victim of a rare disease. None of these are autobiographical summaries of your life starting at birth; rather, they are memoirs about specific time periods or specific situations.

As you write your memoir, you may discover what really happened. You may uncover a secret or two. Readers will recognize themselves in your life. Usually, your memoir reveals a universal truth. For example, Supreme Court Justice Sonia Soto-mayor's memoir, *My Beloved World*, shows the reader that Soto-mayor, in true immigrant fashion, began her American life in a public housing project. She recounts that upon being diagnosed with diabetes as a child, she realized she could not depend upon anyone else, but had to learn to take care of herself and her health needs. That is a defining moment for readers who will remember when they figured out that they, too, must be strong for themselves, when there was no one on whom to depend.

Today's assignment is to look at the following list of words and write one or two sentences about each. Write whatever thoughts, memories, and ideas come into your mind. This list is meant to evoke emotional memories. Please do not reread what you have written until you are finished with the entire list.

- Disappointments
- Accomplishments
- Conflicts
- Fears
- Luck (or lack thereof)
- Enemies
- Gratitude

Now choose whichever topics seem most relevant to you and your life. There's no need to write about a topic that has little meaning to you. The list above may have just a few topics that resonate with you. That's fine. Simply write a few paragraphs, or more if you wish, expanding your thoughts. If you see a connection between today's writing and yesterday's summary of your life, please indicate what that connection is.

Sample

I was criticized a lot when I was a kid. Not only by my mother and my grandmother, but also by the very strict teachers at parochial school. Any little mistake got a punishment. Eventually, I figured out that if I did nothing and never tried I wouldn't get in trouble for making a mistake. That's when I shut up and did not speak in class. So today I'm a grown-up and I don't really know how to participate in life.

This sample is from the writer who on Day 1 wrote, *I'm lonely. But maybe it's my fault because I don't like anybody.* She selected fear as a topic for today, describing how her fear of making a mistake prevents her from socializing, and her fear of being criticized prevents her from speaking when in a group.

Sample

Why is it that my children got along well with all their grandparents but not so much with me and my husband? Generational conflicts are repeating themselves and now we get along with our grandchildren better than they get along with their parents. The grandkids call us and email us and share their news with us and we are happy to listen to them and go places with them. Last summer, we took them on a fabulous trip. I think my daughter might have been jealous.

This is from a travel memoir about a European vacation with grandchildren.

Sample

I had so many fears when I was a kid, it's a wonder I ever left the house. It's a wonder that I wasn't bullied. Actually, I was bullied by my siblings but I don't think you count family bullying. I used to cry in school if an insect flew into the classroom. I used to run to the bathroom to brush my teeth after every meal, even a meal in the school cafeteria. I was afraid of tooth decay. I heard about it from a TV commercial. I was also afraid of halitosis, restless leg syndrome, and ED. The ED commercials really scared me. It wasn't until I was brave enough to ask my parents what that meant that I could breathe a sigh of relief. Girls couldn't get it.

This is part of an essay about the author's phobias. She has written a series of humorous essays, each mocking a different aspect of her childhood personality. When you read personal narratives, you will notice that many writers are self-deprecating and use humor to express serious feelings about serious situations.

When you choose the topic(s) you'll write about, please give the reader plenty of details. Think of several examples of how that topic shaped you. Allow the topic you choose to help you decide what you want the reader to know about your life.

It's important that you write whatever is on your mind. Do not censor yourself. Do not worry about your ability as a writer. Later on, toward the end of the thirty days, you will quickly and easily learn how to polish your writing. For now, the idea is to write and write and write. Your story is original and your story is important. You are the only one who can write your memoir; many people can edit grammar and sentence structure. Do your job now and write, and then write some more. Techniques such as dialogue writing, scene setting, and character development will be taken care of as you proceed through your daily assignments.

Day 3

Search your memory and write a few paragraphs about a time in your life when you were waiting. Maybe you were waiting for something to happen; maybe you were waiting for someone to appear; maybe you were waiting for your feelings to change.

If your thoughts and feelings are positive and happy, you will enhance your memories and your optimism as you recall the pleasant and cheerful aspects of your fortunate life. But, if when you were a child you thought there was no way to escape certain negative feelings, writing now about what your life was really like then will help you understand your past. Perhaps, as you grew older, you realized that you could change your feelings by talking to others and by talking to yourself, by listening to music, by exercising, or by writing. Writing about your thoughts and feelings is a valid psychotherapeutic technique that can actually change the way you react to certain circumstances.

Sample

I can see myself leaning against the brick wall of our apartment building. Waiting. The older girls, they must be about seven or eight, are playing potsy—that's the Bronx version of hopscotch—on the sidewalk right in front of me. They throw their skate keys into each chalk-drawn box and hop around the grid they've created on the concrete. The boys, who are definitely older because they have permission to play in the gutter, are playing punch ball—that's the Bronx no-bat version of softball—with a pink Spaldeen.

You might think it's a typical 1940s spring day, but it's not typical at all. My mother declared today a special day. She's been polishing the furniture and scrubbing the linoleum in our little apartment since dawn. While cleaning, she sings a ditty she's made up: "My husband's coming home. My husband's coming home from the war."

Waiting in front of our building, I'm broadcasting, "My mother's husband is coming home, my mother's husband is coming home from the war," to all passersby. I wonder, what would he look like—this husband?

I see a guy emerge from the Jerome Avenue subway station on the corner. He hoists a green duffel bag over his shoulder. Oh, I guess he's not my mother's husband; he walks right by me and enters our apartment building.

I'm still waiting when he returns a few minutes later with my mother. Is this my mother's husband? My father? I doubt it. I'm almost five years old and I know from the picture books that Miss Marjorie reads to us in nursery school that fathers smoke pipes and wear hats and suits and ties. This guy is wearing a T-shirt and chino pants and he looks too skinny to be a father.

He abruptly lifts me, whirls me, and then says we should go inside. He and my mother hold each other's waists, then they hug, and then they each take one of my hands and together we walk into apartment 1E.

My mother's husband has come home.

In our cozy two rooms, he stares at me and tells me I was a baby when he left. I doubt that. It's been a long time since I was a baby.

Finally, I am brave enough to ask, "Are you my daddy?"

His answer still haunts me.

The above essay about waiting gives the reader much information without explicitly stating facts. The author does not say she was brought up in a city but instead takes us directly to her apartment building and a nearby subway station. At the beginning of the essay, she does not state her age, but instead mentions that she is younger than the seven- and eight-year-olds. She does not name the year but tells us about world happenings during that year. And most important, she does not tell us we will be reading a memoir about a difficult relationship between father and daughter. We surmise that and we are curious to find out what the dad said that still disturbs her. The more the reader is called upon to think, the more engaged the reader becomes with you and your memoir.

Sample

It seems like I spent my whole marriage waiting to have kids. It's all I ever wanted. I wanted to be a dad like my dad was to me. We did so much stuff together and we were a team. I could hardly wait to have a team with my kids. Rebecca said she wanted a family when we were dating, but after we got married she kept saying "Next year, next year." I was relieved when she finally said okay we could start trying, and I was disappointed every month when it turned out she wasn't pregnant. And then the truth came out.

The author gets us interested and we want to read more to find out what that truth was. When you write your sentences and paragraphs to fulfill your daily assignments, use subtlety and give hints to the reader rather than presenting all the facts.

Inspired to write your own memoir? *How to Write a Memoir in 30 Days* gives you the perfect framework. Simple techniques, culled from writers' workshops taught by Dr. Roberta Temes, are presented in a series of fun writing exercises. Everyone has a story to tell. Start writing yours now!

How to Write a Memoir in 30 Days

Step-by-Step Instructions for Creating and Publishing Your Personal Story

Roberta Temes, PhD

ISBN: 978-162145-145-7

Available wherever books are sold.